HIPPOCRENE HANDY DICTIONARIES

Japanese

MW00764062

HIPPOCRENE HANDY DICTIONARIES

For the traveler of independent spirit and curious mind, this practical series will help you to communicate, not just get by. Easier to use than a dictionary, the comprehensive listing of words and phrases is arranged alphabetically by key word. More versatile than a phrasebook, words frequently met in stores, on signs, or needed for standard replies, are conveniently presented by subject.

ARABIC
ISBN 0-87052-960-9

PORTUGUESE
ISBN 0-87052-053-9

CHINESE
ISBN 0-87052-050-4

RUSSIAN
ISBN 0-7818-0013-7

DUTCH
ISBN 0-87052-049-0

SERBO-CROATIAN
ISBN 0-87052-051-2

FRENCH
ISBN 0-7818-0010-2

SLOVAK
ISBN 0-7818-0101-1

GERMAN
ISBN 0-7818-0014-5

SPANISH
ISBN 0-7818-0012-9

GREEK
ISBN 0-87052-961-7

SWEDISH
ISBN 0-87052-054-7

ITALIAN
ISBN 0-7818-0011-0

THAI
ISBN 0-87052-963-3

JAPANESE
ISBN 0-87052-962-5

TURKISH
ISBN 0-87052-982-X

KOREAN
ISBN 0-7818-0082-X

Books may be ordered directly from the publisher. Each book costs $6.95. Send the total amount plus $3.50 for
Hippocrene Books, Inc.
171 Madison Avenue
New York, NY 10016.

HIPPOCRENE HANDY DICTIONARIES

Japanese

compiled by

LEXUS

with

Mami Crocket
Keiko Holmes
and
Anthony P. Newell

HIPPOCRENE BOOKS
New York

Published in the United States of America in 1991 by
HIPPOCRENE BOOKS, INC., New York,
by arrangement with Routledge, London

For information, address:
HIPPOCRENE BOOKS, INC.
171 Madison Ave.
New York, NY 10016

ISBN 0-87052-962-5

Contents

PRONUNCIATION GUIDE

Since Japanese is normally written in a form of script all its own, one which requires a great deal of study, we have used a system of transliteration which will make the spoken Japanese language readily accessible.

There are already in popular use a number of systems which 'romanize' Japanese, but these systems all have the failing of tending to represent the structure of Japanese words at the expense of the sound that these Japanese words have when actually spoken. For example, many systems give 'desu' or 'shita' for words that actually sound like 'dess' or 'shta'. Because the latter pair represent the way these words *really* sound, that is how they appear in this book. If an English speaker, bearing the following simple points in mind, pronounces the words as though they were English, the result will be clearly comprehensible to a Japanese person.

1. *Stress.* To all intents and purposes there is no stress in Japanese. So give the same value to all syllables: say 'Yo-ko-ha-ma' not 'Yo-ko-HAR-ma'.

2. *Vowels.* There are only five vowel sounds in Japanese:

a	as in 'part' (but shorter)	o	as in 'port' (but shorter)
e	as in 'pet'	u	as in 'put'
i	as in 'peat' (but shorter)		

Remember that there are no silent letters. So when 'e', for example, comes at the end of a word it must be pronounced: 'are' is 'ah-reh' (not as in 'are' in English!).

A bar line over a vowel indicates that the vowel is twice as long as one without a bar line. Distinguish carefully between 'oba-san' (aunt) and 'obā-san' (grandmother), etc.

Vowels often appear in combination, but always retain their basic sound:

ai	sounds like 'eye'
ae	sounds like 'ah-eh'
ei	sounds like the 'ay' of 'pay'

3. *Consonants.*

g	as in 'go'
j	as in 'jar'
y	as in 'yet'

Note that 'y' is never a long 'i' sound. For example, the 'Kyū' of 'Kyūshū' is like the 'cu' of 'cute' and never like the 'ki' of 'kite'.

The letter 'r' can sound like an 'l' or even a 'd'. Although an English-type 'r' is acceptable, it will sound nearer the mark if you tap the tip of your tongue against the ridge behind your upper front teeth.

Double consonants, like double vowels, are an important feature of Japanese and have been hyphenated in this book to remind the reader to keep them double. The difference between the 'n's of 'ana' (hole) and 'an-na' (that kind of) is like the difference between the 'n's of 'benefit' and 'Ben Nevis'. The same applies to hyphenation at the end of a word, for example 'kip-p'. In such cases, hold the sound momentarily, then release the sound with its full value (don't swallow the '-p').

n': Make a slight break between the 'n" and the following sound.
(no), (na): for an explanation of this see the Reference Grammar (page 111).

English-Japanese

A

a (*one*) hitots (no); **100 yen a bottle** ip-pon hyaku-en; *see page 99*

abacus soroban

abalone awabi

about: about 25 nijū-go kurai; **about 30 years of age** sanjiss-sai kurai; **about 6 o'clock** roku-ji goro; **about noon** hiru goro; **is the manager about?** manējā wa irash-shai-mass ka?; **I was just about to leave** watashi wa chōdo deru tokoro deshta; **how about a drink?** chot-to nomi-masen ka?

above ue; **above the village** mura no ue

abroad gaikok

abscess haremono

absolutely: it's absolutely perfect mat-taku kanzen dess; **you're absolutely right** mat-tak sono tōri dess; **absolutely!** sō dess ne!

absorbent cotton dash-shimen

accelerator akseru

accept (*present*) uketoru; **please accept this present** kono purezento o uketot-te kudasai

accident jiko; **there's been an accident** jiko ga ari-mashta; **sorry, it was an accident** sumi-masen, waza to ja ari-masen deshta

accommodation(s) heya; **we need accommodation(s) for four** yonim-bun heya ga iri-mass

accurate seikak (na)

ache: I have an ache here koko ga itami-mass; **it aches** itami-mass

across: across the street michi no mukō-gawa

actor haiyū

actress joyū

adapter (*electrical*) adaptā

address jūsho; **what's your address?** gojūsho wa?

address book jūsho-rok

admission nyūjōryō; **how much is admission?** nyūjōryō wa ikura dess ka?

adore: I adore ... (*this country, this food etc*) ... ga daiski dess

adult otona

advance: in advance mae mot-te; **I'll pay in advance** mae mot-te harai-mass

advertisement senden

advise: what would you advise? nanika adobaiss ga ari-mass ka?

aeroplane hikōki

affluent yūhuk (na)

afraid: I'm afraid of ... ... ga kowai dess; **don't be afraid** kowagaranaide kudasai; **I'm not afraid** kowaku ari-masen; **I'm afraid I can't help you** sumi-masen ga, tetsdae-masen; **I'm afraid so** zan-nen-nagara sō dess; **I'm afraid not** zan-nen-nagara dame dess

after ato de; **after dinner** yūshok no ato de; **after 9 o'clock** ku-ji sugi; **not until after 9 o'clock** ku-ji sugi made dame dess; **after you** dōzo osaki ni

afternoon gogo; **in the afternoon** gogo; **good afternoon** kon-nichi wa; **this afternoon** kyō no gogo

aftershave ahutā-shēb

aftersun cream hiyake kurīm

afterwards ato de

again mata

against (*opposed to*) hantai (no); **I'm against it** sore ni wa hantai dess

age toshi; **under age** miseinen; **not at my age!** toshigai mo nak!; **it takes ages** nagaku kakari-mass; **I haven't been here for ages** zuibun nagaku koko ni wa ki-masen deshta

agency dairi-ten

aggressive kōgeki-teki (na)

ago mae; **a year ago** ichinem-mae; **it**

wasn't long ago son-na ni mae no koto ja ari-masen

agony: it's agony kurushī!

agree: do you agree? anata mo sō omoi-mass ka?; **I agree** dōkan dess; **would you like some sea cucumber? — no, it doesn't agree with me** namako wa ikaga dess ka? — īe, taberare-masen

AIDS eidz

air kūki; **I want some fresh air** shinsen na kūki ga hoshī dess; **by air** (travel) hikōki de; (send) kōkūbin de; **I'm going by air** hikōki de iki-mass; **I'll send it by air** kōkūbin de okuri-mass

air-conditioning eya-kon

air hostess eya-hostess

airmail: by airmail kōkūbin de

airmail envelope kōkūbin'yō hūtō

airplane hikōki

airport kūkō

airport bus eyapōto bass

airport tax kūkō-zei

à la carte ara karuto

alarm keihō

alarm clock mezamash-dokei

alcohol arukōru

alcoholic: is it alcoholic? arukōru ga hait-te i-mass ka?

alcove tokonoma

alive ikite; **is he still alive?** kare wa mada ikite i-mass ka?

all zembu; **all the hotels** zembu no hoteru; **all my friends** watashi no tomodachi zembu; **all my money** arigane zembu; **all of it** zembu; **all of them** zembu; **all right** ī dess; **I'm all right** daijōbu dess; **that's all** sore dake dess; **it's all changed** zembu kawari-mashta; **thank you — not at all** arigatō — dō itashi-mashte

allergic: I'm allergic to ... watashi wa ... arerugī dess

allergy arerugī

all-inclusive zembu hukumete

allowed yurusareta; **is smoking allowed?** tabako o sut-te ī dess ka?; **I'm not allowed to eat salt** watashi wa shio wa taberare-masen

almost hotondo

alone hitori; **I'm going alone** hitori de iki-mass; **are you alone?** ohitori

dess ka?; **leave me alone** kamawanaide kudasai

Alps Arups

already sude ni

also mo; **I also want to see Himeji Castle** shirasagi-jō mo mi-tai dess

alteration henkō

alternative: is there an alternative? hoka ni yari-yō ga ari-masen ka?; **we had no alternative** hoka ni yari-yō ga ari-masen deshta

altogether zembu de; **what does that come to altogether?** zembu de ikura dess ka?

always itsmo

a.m.: at 8 a.m. gozen hachi-ji ni; *see page 117*

amazing subarashī

ambassador taishi

ambulance kyūkyū-sha; **get an ambulance!** kyūkyū-sha o yonde kudasai!

America Amerika

American (*adjective*) Amerika (no); (*person*) Amerika-jin; **the Americans** Amerika-jin

American plan shokuji-tski

among: among ourselves watashtachi no aida de

amp: a 5 amp fuse go-ampeya no hyūz

an(a)esthetic masui

ancestor senzo

ancient kodai (no)

and (*with nouns*) to; **Tokyo and London** Tōkyō to Rondon; (*with phrases*) soshte; **we stayed in Nara for 3 days and went to Kyoto** Nara ni mik-ka ite soshte Kyōto e iki-mashta; (*at the beginning of a sentence*) sorekara; **and me too** sorekara watashi mo

angina kyōshin-shō

angry okot-ta; **I'm very angry about it** watashi wa sono koto de hontō ni okot-te i-mass

animal dōbuts

ankle ashkubi

anniversary: it's our (wedding) anniversary today kyō wa watashtachi no (kek-kon) kinembi dess

annoy: he's annoying me kare wa

watashi o komarasete i-mass; **it's so annoying** komat-ta ne!
anorak anorak-k
another: can we have another room? betsu no heya ga ari-mass ka?; **another bottle, please** mō ip-pon' onegai-shi-mass
answer: there was no answer henji ga ari-masen deshta; **what was his answer?** kare no kotae wa dō deshta ka?
ant: ants ari
antibiotics kōsei-bush-shits
anticlimax kitai-hazure
antifreeze hutō-eki
antihistamine kō-histamin-zai
antique kot-tō-hin; **is it an antique?** sore wa kot-tō-hin dess ka?
antique shop kot-tō-ten
antisocial: don't be antisocial tskiai ga warui dess ne
any: have you got any rolls? rōru-pan ga ari-mass ka?; **have you got any milk?** miruk ga ari-mass ka?; **I haven't got any** zenzen' ari-masen
anybody dare ka; **can anybody help?** dare ka tetsdat-te kure-masen ka?; **there wasn't anybody there** soko ni wa dare mo i-masen deshta
anything nani ka; **I don't want anything** nani mo hoshku ari-masen; **don't you have anything else?** hoka ni nani ka ari-masen ka?
apart: apart from ... ... igai de wa
apartment apāto
apology shazai; **please accept my apologies** hontō ni sumi-masen deshta
appalling hidoi
appear: it would appear that ... ... yō ni mie-mass
appendicitis mōchō-en
appetite shoku-yok; **I've lost my appetite** shoku-yoku o nakshi-mashta
apple rin-go
apple pie ap-puru pai
application form mōshkomi-yōshi
appointment yoyak; **I'd like to make an appointment** yoyak shtain dess
appreciate: thank you, I appreciate it hontō ni arigatō gozai-mass
approve: she doesn't approve kanojo wa sansei shi-masen

April shi-gats
arch(a)eology kōkogak
are *see pages 108, 111*
area chīki; **I don't know the area** sono chīki o shiri-masen
area code shigai-kyokuban
arm ude
around *see* **about**
arranged marriage omiai kek-kon
arrangement tehai; **will you make the arrangements?** tehai shte kure-masen ka?
arrest taiho suru; **he's been arrested** kare wa taiho sarete i-mass
arrival tōchak
arrive tsku; **when do we arrive?** its tski-mass ka?; **has my parcel arrived yet?** watashi no nimots wa mada tski-masen ka?; **let me know as soon as they arrive** tski shidai shirasete kudasai; **we only arrived yesterday** kinō tsuita bakari dess
art bijuts
art gallery bijuts-kan
arthritis kansetsu-en
artificial jinkō (no)
artist geijuts-ka
as: as fast as you can dekiru dake hayak; **as much as you can** dekiru dake taksan; **as you like** oski na yō ni; **as it's getting late** mō osoi node
ashore: to go ashore jōrik suru
ashtray haizara
Asia Ajia
Asian (*adjective*) Ajia (no); (*person*) Ajia-jin
aside: aside from ... ... igai de wa
ask tanomu; **that's not what I asked for** sore wa tanonda no ja ari-masen; **could you ask him to phone me back?** kare ni denwa o kureru yō tanonde kure-masen ka?; **let's ask the policeman over there** asoko no omawari-san ni kiki-mashō
asleep: he's still asleep kare wa mada nemut-te i-mass
asparagus asparagass
aspirin aspirin
assault: she's been assaulted kanojo wa osoware-mashta; **indecent assault** waisets kōi
assistant (*helper*) joshu; (*in shop*) ten'in
assume: I assume that ... ... to omoi-

mass
asthma zensok
astonishing odoroku-yō (na)
at: at the café kiss-saten de; **at the hotel** hoteru de; **at 8 o'clock** hachi-ji ni; **see you at dinner** yūshok no toki ai-mashō
Atlantic Taisei-yō
atmosphere hun'iki
attractive miryok-teki; **you're very attractive** anata wa totemo kirei dess
aubergine nass
auction kyōbai
audience chōshū
August hachi-gats
aunt oba-san; **my aunt** oba
Australia Ōstoraria
Australian (*adjective*) Ōstoraria (no); (*person*) Ōstoraria-jin; **the Australians** Ōstoraria-jin
authorities tōkyok
automatic jidō

automobile jidōsha
autumn aki; **in the autumn** aki ni
available: when will it be available? its te ni hairi-mass ka?; **when will he be available?** kare ni itsu ae-mass ka?
avalanche nadare
avenue ōdōri
average: the average Japanese hutsū no Nihon-jin; **an above average hotel** hyōjun'ijō no hoteru; **a below average hotel** hyōjun'ika no hoteru; **the food was only average** shokuji wa hutsū deshta; **on average** heikin shte
awake okite; **is she awake?** kanojo wa okite i-mass ka?
away: is it far away? tōi dess ka?; **go away!** at-chi e it-te!
awful osoroshī
axle shajik
azalea tsutsuji

B

baby akachan
baby-carrier akachan no kago
baby-sitter bebī-shit-tā; **can you get us a baby-sitter?** bebī-shit-tā o sagashte kure-masen ka?
bachelor dokshin
back (*of body*) senaka; **I've got a bad back** senaka ga warui dess; **at the back** ushiro ni; **in the back of the car** kuruma no ushiro ni; **I'll be right back** sugu modori-mass; **when do you want it back?** its kaeshi-mashō ka?; **can I have my money back?** okane o kaeshte kure-masen ka?; **come back!** modot-te kite kudasai!; **I go back home tomorrow** ashta uchi e kaeri-mass; **we'll be back next year** watashtachi wa rainen kaet-te ki-mass; **when is the last bus back?** kaeri no saishū bass wa nan-ji dess ka?
backache: I have a backache senaka

ga itami-mass
back door ura no doa
backpack ryuk-k sak-k
back seat ushiro no seki
back street ura-dōri
bacon bēkon; **bacon and eggs** bēkon'eg-g
bad warui; **this meat's bad** kono nik wa ksat-te i-mass; **a bad headache** hidoi zutsū; **it's not bad** māmā dess; **too bad!** zan-nen dess ne!
badly: he's been badly injured kare wa hidoku kega shi-mashta
bag kaban; (*paper bag*) hukuro; (*carrier bag*) binīru-bukuro; (*suitcase*) sūtskèss
baggage tenimots
baggage allowance tenimots jūryō-seigen
baggage checkroom tenimotsu azukarisho
bakery pan'ya
balcony barukonī; **a room with a**

balcony barukonī no aru heya; **on the balcony** barukonī de
bald hageta
ball bōru
ballet barē
ball-point pen bōru-pen
bamboo take; **bamboo shoots** takenoko
banana banana
band (*music*) bando
bandage hōtai; **could you change the bandage?** hōtai o kaete kure-masen ka?
bandaid bandoēdo
bank ginkō; **when are the banks open?** ginkō wa nan ji ni aki-mass ka?
bank account kōza
banker ginkōka
bar bā; **let's meet in the bar** bā de ai-mashō; **a bar of chocolate** itachoko
barbecue bābekyū
barber (*shop*) toko-ya
bargain: it's a real bargain kai-dok dess
barmaid jokyū
barman bāten
barrette hea-kurip-p
bartender bāten
baseball yakyū
basic: the hotel is rather basic kono hoteru ni wa tokubets na mono wa nani mo ari-masen; **will you teach me some basic phrases?** kihon-teki na kotoba o oshiete kure-masen ka?
basket kago
basketball basket-to bōru
bath ohuro; **can I take a bath?** ohuro ni hait-te mo ī dess ka?; **could you give me a bath towel?** taoru o kudasai-masen ka?
bathing nyū-yok; (*swimming*) suiei
bathing costume kai-sui-gi
bathrobe bass-rōb
bathroom ohuro-ba; **a room with a private bathroom** bass-tski no heya; **can I use your bathroom?** toire o tskat-te mo ī dess ka?
battery (*cell*) denchi; (*in car*) bat-terī; **the battery's flat** (*cell*) denchi ga nakunari-mashta; (*in car*) bat-terī ga agat-te shimai-mashta

bay wan; **Tokyo Bay** Tōkyō-wan
be: be reasonable mucha na koto o it-te wa ike-masen; **don't be lazy** namakenaide kudasai; **where have you been?** doko e it-te i-mashta ka?; **I've never been to Kyoto** Kyōto e it-ta koto wa ari-masen; *see page 108*
beach hama; **on the beach** hama de; **I'm going to the beach** hama e iki-mass
beads bīdz
beans mame
bear kuma
beard hige
beautiful (*person*) kirei (na); (*meal*) oishī; (*holiday*) subarashī; **thank you, that's beautiful** arigatō, totemo subarashī dess
beauty salon biyōin
because kara; **because I don't understand Japanese** Nihon-go ga wakari-masen kara; **because of the weather** tenkō no sei de
bed (*Western-style*) bed-do; (*Japanese-style*) nedoko; **single bed** shin-guru bed-do; **double bed** daburu bed-do; **you haven't made my bed** watashi no bed-do o naoshte i-masen; **could you lay my bed out?** nedoko o shīte kudasai; **he's still in bed** kare wa mada bed-do ni i-mass; **I'm going to bed** mō ne-mass
bed and breakfast chōshok-tski yado
bed linen shīts-rui
bedroom shinshits
bee mitsbachi
beef gyūnik
beer bīru; **two beers, please** bīru ni-hai onegai-shi-mass
before mae ni; **before breakfast** chōshok no mae ni; **before I leave** deru mae ni; **I haven't been here before** koko ni kita koto wa ari-masen
begin: when does it begin? its hajimari-mass ka?
beginner shoshin-sha; **I'm just a beginner** watashi wa shoshin-sha dess
beginning: at the beginning hajime ni
behavio(u)r taido; **his behavio(u)r** kare no taido; **his behavio(u)r**

towards me kare no watashi ni taisuru taido

behind ushiro; **the driver behind me** watashi no ushiro no untenshu

beige bēju-iro

believe: I don't believe you shinjirare-masen; **I believe you** anata o shinji-mass

bell beru; (*in temple*) kane; (*wind chimes*) hūrin

belong: that belongs to me watashi no dess; **who does this belong to?** kore wa dare no dess ka?

belongings: all my belongings watashi no mono zembu

below (*under*) shta; **below the knee** hiza no shta; (*less than*) ika; **below the average** heikin'ika

belt (*clothing*) beruto

bend (*in road*) kāb

berries berī

berth shindai

beside: beside the church kyōkai no soba ni; **sit beside me** watashi no soba ni suwat-te kudasai

besides: besides that sore igai ni

best saikō (no); **the best hotel in town** machi de˙saikō no hoteru; **that's the best meal I've ever had** watashi ga tabeta ryōri no uchi de saikō dess

bet: I bet you 5000 yen go-sen'en kake-mass

better mot-to ī; **that's better!** sono hō ga ī; **are you feeling better?** kibun ga yok nari-mashta ka?; **I'm feeling a lot better** kibun ga zut-to yok nari-mashta; **I'd better be going now** mō soro-soro ikanakereba

between: between ... ... no aida ni

beyond no mukō ni; **beyond the mountains** yama no mukō ni

bicycle jitensha; **can we rent bicycles here?** koko ni kashi-jitensha ga ari-mass ka?

big ōkī; **a big one** ōkī no; **that's too big** ōki-sugi-mass; **it's not big enough** chīsa-sugi-mass

bigger mot-to ōkī

bike jitensha

bikini bikini

bill okanjō; **could I have the bill, please?** okanjō onegai-shi-mass

billfold saihu

billiards biriyādo

bird tori

biro (*tm*) bōru-pen

birthday tanjōbi; **it's my birthday** watashi no tanjōbi dess; **when is your birthday?** otanjōbi wa its dess ka?; **happy birthday!** otanjōbi omedetō gozai-mass

biscuit bisket-to

bit: just a little bit for me hon no skoshi dake; **a big bit** ōkī no; **a bit of that cake, please** sono kēki o skoshi onegai-shi-mass; **it's a bit too big for me** chot-to ōki-sugi-mass; **it's a bit cold today** kyō wa chot-to samui dess

bite kamu; **I've been bitten** kamaremashta; **do you have something for bites?** mush-sasare no ksuri ga ari-mass ka?

bitter (*taste*) nigai

bitter lemon bitā remon

black kuro; **black and white film** (*for camera*) shiro-kuro firum

blackout: he's had a blackout kare wa kizets shi-mashta

bladder bōkō

blanket mōhu; **I'd like another blanket** mō ichi-mai mōhu o kuremasen ka?

blazer burezā

bleed shuk-kets suru; **he's bleeding** kare wa shuk-kets shte i-mass

bless you! (*after sneeze*) *the Japanese have no equivalent for this*

blind mōjin (no)

blinds buraindo

blind spot (*driving*) mitōshi no warui tokoro

blister mizubukure

blocked (*road, drain*) husagareta

block of flats ik-ken no apāto

blond (*adjective*) kimpats (no)

blonde (*woman*) burondo

blood ketsu-eki; **his blood group is ...** kare no ketsu-eki-gata wa ...; **I have high blood pressure** watashi wa kōketsu-ats dess

bloody mary uok-ka-iri tomato-jūss

blouse burauss

blue aoi

blusher (*cosmetic*) hōbeni

board: full board sanshok-tski; **half-**

board chōshok to yūshok tski
boarding house geshku
boarding pass tōjō-ken
boat (*small, rowing*) bōto; (*large, cargo, passenger*) hune
body karada; (*of car*) shatai
boil (*on body*) haremono; **boil the water please** oyu o wakashte kudasai
boiled egg yude tamago
boiled rice gohan
boiling hot (*weather, food*) totemo atsui
bomb (*noun*) bakudan
bone (*in meat, body, fish*) hone
bonnet (*of car*) bon-net-to
bonus bōnass
book (*noun*) hon; (*verb*) yoyak suru; **I'd like to book a table for two** hutari-bun no tēburu no yoyaku o onegai-shi-mass
bookshop, bookstore hon'ya
boot (*on foot*) būts; (*of car*) kuruma no torank
booze sake; **I had too much booze** sake o nomi-sugi-mashta
border (*of country*) kok-kyō
bored: I'm bored taikuts dess
boring (*person, trip, film*) taikuts (na)
born: I was born in ... (*date*) ... ni umare-mashta; (*place*) ... de umare-mashta
borrow: may I borrow ...? ... o kashte kure-masen ka?
boss boss
both ryōhō; **I'll take both of them** ryōhō hoshī dess; **we'll both come** hutari-tomo iki-mass
bother: sorry to bother you sumi-masen; **it's no bother** chit-tomo kamai-masen yo; **it's such a bother** hontō ni mendō dess
bottle bin; **a bottle of wine** wain' ip-pon; **another bottle, please** mō ip-pon' onegai-shi-mass
bottle-opener sen-nuki
bottom soko; **at the bottom of the sea/box** umi/hako no soko ni; **at the bottom of the hill** oka no humoto ni
bottom gear rō-giya
bouncer (*at club*) yōjimbō
bowels chō
bowling bōring-g
box hako

box lunch bentō
box office kip-pu uriba
boy otoko no ko
boyfriend: my boyfriend watashi no bōi-hurendo
bra brajā
bracelet udewa
brake fluid burēki-eki
brakes burēki; **there's something wrong with the brakes** burēki no chōshi ga okashī dess; **can you check the brakes?** burēki o shirabete kure-masen ka?; **I had to brake suddenly** kyūteisha shinakereba nari-masen deshta
brandy burandē
brave yūkan (na)
bread pan; **could we have some bread and butter?** batā-tski pan'o kure-masen ka?; **some more bread, please** mot-to pan'o kure-masen ka?; **white bread** shiro-pan; **brown bread** kuro-pan; **wholemeal bread** muhyōhak pan; **rye bread** raimugi-pan
break kowass; **I think I've broken my ankle** dōmo ashkubi o ot-ta yō dess; **it keeps breaking** shot-chū koware-mass
breakdown: I've had a breakdown kuruma ga enko shi-mashta; **nervous breakdown** shinkei-suijak
breakfast chōshok; **English/full breakfast** huru kōss chōshok; **Japanese breakfast** wa-shki chōshok; **continental breakfast** yō-shki chōshok
break in: somebody's broken in akiss ni yarare-mashta
breast (*chest*) mune; (*bosom*) chibusa
breast-feed bonyū de sodateru
breath iki; **out of breath** iki o kirashte
breathe iki o suru; **I can't breathe** iki ga deki-masen
breathtaking subarashī
breeze soyokaze
breezy: a breezy day kaze no aru hi; **it's breezy today** kyō wa soyokaze ga ari-mass
bridal suite shinkom-beya
bride hanayome
bridegroom hanamuko
bridge (*over river*) hashi

brief (*stay*, *visit*) mijikai
briefcase burīhu-kēss
bright (*colour*) azayaka (na); **bright red** azayaka na aka; (*dazzling*) mabushī
brilliant (*idea*) subarashī; (*colour*) hanayaka (na)
bring mot-te kuru; **could you bring it to my hotel?** hoteru made mot-te kite kure-masen ka?; **I'll bring it back** kaeshi ni ki-mass; **can I bring a friend too?** tomodachi mo tsurete kite ī dess ka?
Britain Eikok
British Eikok (no); **the British** Eikok-jin
brochure pamhuret-to; **do you have any brochures on ...?** ... no pamhuret-to ga ari-mass ka?
broke: I'm broke ichi mon nashi dess
broken kowareta; **you've broken it** anata ga kowashi-mashta; **it's broken** kowarete i-mass
broken nose oreta hana
brooch burōchi
brother (*elder*) onī-san; **my elder brother** ani; (*younger*) otōto-san; **my younger brother** otōto
brother-in-law (*elder*) giri no onī-san; **my elder brother-in-law** giri no ani; (*younger*) giri no otōto-san; **my younger brother-in-law** giri no otōto
brown cha-iro; **I don't go brown** kurok nari-masen
browse: may I just browse around? mite mawaru dake demo ī dess ka?
bruise (*noun*) dabok-shō
brunette burunet-to
brush (*noun*) burash
bucket bakets
Buddha hotoke-sama
Buddhism buk-kyō
Buddhist (*adjective*) buk-kyō (no); (*noun*) buk-kyō-to
buffet byuf-fe
bug (*insect*) mushi; **she's caught a bug** kanojo wa byōki dess
building biru
bulb (*electrical*) denkyū; **a new bulb** atarashī denkyū
bull oushi
bullet train shinkansen
bump: I bumped my head atama o uchi-mashta
bumper bampā
bumpy (*road*) dekoboko (no)
bunch of flowers hana-taba
bungalow hiraya
bunion oyayubi-katsueki-nōshu
bunk nedana
bunk beds ni-dam bed-do
buoy bui
burglar dorobō
burn: do you have an ointment for burns? yakedo no ksuri ga ari-mass ka?
burnt: this meat is burnt kono nik wa kogete i-mass; **my arms are so burnt** ude ga totemo hi ni yake-mashta
burst: a burst pipe harets shta paip
bus bass; **is this the bus for ...?** kore wa ... iki no bass dess ka?; **when's the next bus?** tsugi no bass wa nan-ji dess ka?
bus driver bass no untenshu
business shigoto; **I'm here on business** shigoto de ki-mashta; **it's a pleasure to do business with you** anata to shigoto ga dekite, ureshī dess
business hotel bijiness hoteru
businessman bijiness-man; (*white collar worker*) sararī-man
business woman bijiness ūman
bus station bass no tāminaru
bus stop bass-tei; **will you tell me which bus stop I get off at?** dono bass-tei de oritara ī ka oshiete kure-masen ka?
bust (*of body*) basto
bus tour bass tsuā
busy (*street*, *restaurant*) konda; **I'm busy this evening** kon'ya wa isogashī dess; **the line was busy** (*telephone*) hanash-chū deshta
but demo; **not ... but ...** ... de nakte ... dess
butcher nikuya
butter batā
butterfly chōchō
button botan
buy: I'll buy it kai-mass; **where can I buy ...?** doko de ... ga kae-mass ka?
by: by train densha de; **by car** kuruma de; **by boat** hune de;

who's it written by? dare ga kaki-mashta ka?; **a novel by Mishima** Mishima no kaita shōsets; **I came by myself** hitori de ki-mashta; **a seat by the window** mado giwa no seki; **by the sea** umi no soba; **can you do it by Wednesday?** suiyōbi made ni deki-mass ka?

bye-bye sayonara

bypass (*road*) bai-pass

C

cab (*taxi*) takshī

cabaret kyabarē

cabbage kyabets

cabin (*on ship*) senshits; (*in mountains*) yama-goya

cable (*electrical*) kēburu

cablecar kēburukā

café kiss-saten

caffeine kafein

cake kēki; **a piece of cake** kēki hito-kire

calculator keisanki

calendar karendā

call: what is this called? kore wa nan to ī-mass ka?; **call the manager!** shihainin' o yonde kudasai!; **I'd like to make a call to England** Igiriss ni denwa shtai dess; **I'll call back later** (*come back*) mata ato de ki-mass; (*phone back*) mata ato de denwa shi-mass; **I'm expecting a call from London** Rondon kara no denwa o mat-te i-mass; **would you give me a call at 7.30?** shchi-ji-han ni denwa shte kure-masen ka?; **it's been called off** enki ni nari-mashta

call box kōshū denwa

calligraphy shodō

calm (*person, sea*) shizka (na); **calm down!** ochitski nasai!

calories karorī

camelia tsubaki

camera kamera

can (*tin*) kanzume; **a can of beer** kan'iri bīru

can: can I ...? ...-te ī dess ka?; **can you ...?** ... koto ga deki-mass ka?; **can he ...?** kare wa ... koto ga deki-mass ka?; **can we ...?** ...-te ī dess ka?; **can they ...?** karera wa ... koto ga deki-mass ka?; **I can't ... ...** koto ga deki-masen; **he can't ...** kare wa ... koto ga deki-masen; **can I keep it?** morat-te mo ī dess ka?; **if I can** moshi dekireba; **that can't be right** son-na haz ga ari-masen; *see page 107*

Canada Kanada

Canadian (*adjective*) Kanada (no); (*person*) Kanada-jin

cancel torikess; **can I cancel my reservation?** yoyaku o torikesh-tain dess ga; **can we cancel dinner for tonight?** komban no yūshoku o torikeshte kure-masen ka?; **I cancelled it** torikeshi-mashta

cancellation torikeshi

candle rōsok

candies kyandē; **a piece of candy** kyandē hitots

canoe kanū

can-opener kan-kiri

cap (*to wear*) bōshi; **bathing cap** suiei-bō

capital city shuto

capsize: it capsized tempuk shi-mashta

captain (*of ship*) senchō

car kuruma

carafe mizusashi

carat: is it (9/14 carat) gold? sore wa (kyū karat-to no/jūyon karat-to no) kin dess ka?

carbonated tansan'iri (no)

carburet(t)or kyaburetā

card (*name card*) meishi; **do you have a card?** meishi o omochi dess ka?; (*New Year Card*) nen-

ga-jō
cardboard box dambōru-bako
cardigan kādigan
cards toramp; **do you play cards?**
torampu o shi-mass ka?
care: goodbye, take care sayonara, ki
o tskete; **will you take care of this
bag for me?** kono kaban' o mite-ite
kure-masen ka?; **care of ... ...** kata
careful: be careful ki o tskete
careless: that was careless of you
huchūi deshta ne; **careless driving**
huchūi unten
car ferry kā ferī
car hire renta kā
car keys kuruma no kagi
carnation kānēshon
carnival kānibaru
car park chūshajō
carp koi
carpet jūtan
carp streamer koinobori
car rental renta kā
carrot ninjin
carry mots; **could you carry this for
me?** kore o mot-te kure-mass ka?
carry-all ōkina tesage-bukuro
car-sick: I get car-sick kuruma ni
yoi-mass
carton kāton; **a carton of milk**
miruku ichi-kāton
cartoon film animēshon
carving chōkok
carwash sensha
case (*suitcase*) sūts-kēss; **in any case**
izureni shtemo; **in that case** sono bāi
ni wa; **it's a special case** sore wa
tokubets dess; **in case he comes
back** kare ga kaet-te kitara; **I'll take
two just in case** yōjin no tame ni
hutats mot-te iki-mass
cash genkin; **I don't have any cash**
genkin wa zenzen' ari-masen; **I'll
pay cash** genkin de harai-mass; **will
you cash a cheque/check for me?**
kogit-te o genkin ni shte kure-masen
ka?
cashdesk kaikei gakari
cash dispenser genkin jidō
madoguchi
cash register reji
cassette kaset-to
cassette player, cassette recorder

kaset-to rekōdā
castle shiro; **Osaka Castle** Ōsaka-jō
casual: casual clothes hudan-gi
cat neko
catastrophe dai-saigai
catch: where do we catch the bus?
doko de bass ni nori-mass ka?; **he's
caught some strange illness** kare wa
wake no wakaranai byōki ni kakat-te
i-mass
catching: is it catching? utsuri-yasui
dess ka?
Catholic (*adjective*) Katorik-k (no)
cauliflower karihurawā
cause gen'in
cave hora-ana
caviar kyabia
cedar sugi
ceiling tenjō
celebrations shkugakai
celery serori
cellophane serohan
Celsius sesh-shi; *see page 121*
cemetery bochi
center chūshin; *see also* **centre**
centigrade sesh-shi; *see page 121*
centimetre, centimeter senchi; *see
page 119*
central chūshin (no); **we'd prefer
something more central** mot-to
benri na tokoro ga ī dess
central heating sentoraru hīting-g
central station chūō-eki
centre chūshin; **how do we get to the
centre?** chūshin-chi ni wa dō iki-
mass ka?; **in the centre (of town)**
machi no chūshin ni
century seiki; **in the 19th/20th
century** jūkyū/nijū seiki ni
ceramics setomono
ceremony (*tea ceremony*) chanoyu;
(*opening ceremony*) kaikai-shki
certain tashka; **are you certain?**
tashka dess ka?; **I'm absolutely
certain** hontō ni tashka dess
certainly tashka ni; **certainly not** (*that
is wrong*) zet-tai chigai-mass; (*I refuse*)
dame dess!
certificate shōmeisho; **birth certificate**
koseki tōhon
chain (*for bike, around neck*) ksari
chair iss
chambermaid meido-san

champagne shampen

chance: quite by chance hon no gūzen de; **no chance!** mikomi wa ari-masen!

change: could you change this into yen? kore o en ni kaete kure-masen ka?; **I haven't got any change** komakai okane wa ari-masen; **can you give me change for a 10,000 yen note?** ichi-man'en de otsuri ga ari-mass ka?; **do we have to change (trains)?** norikae shinakereba nari-masen ka?; **for a change** kibun'o kaeru tame ni; **you haven't changed the sheets** shītsu o kaete i-masen; **the place has changed so much** zuibun kawat-te shimai-mashta; **do you want to change places with me?** seki o kawari-mashō ka?; **can I change this for ...?** kore o ... ni kaete kure-masen ka?

changeable (*weather*) kawari-yasui

chaos dai-konran

chap hito; **the chap at reception** uketske no hito

chapel chaperu

character (*written*) ji; **in Japanese characters** Nihon-go de

charge: is there an extra charge? hoka ni harau koto ga ari-mass ka?; **what do you charge?** ikura dess ka?; **who's in charge here?** koko no sekinin-sha wa dare dess ka?

charming miryokteki (na)

charter flight chātā-bin

chassis shashī

cheap yasui; **do you have something cheaper?** mot-to yasui no wa ari-masen ka?

cheat: I've been cheated damasare-mashta

check: will you check? shirabete kure-masen ka?; **will you check the steering?** stearing-gu o shirabete kure-masen ka?; **will you check the bill?** seikyūsho o shirabete kure-masen ka?; **I've checked it** mō shirabe-mashta

check (*financial*) kogit-te; **will you take a check?** kogit-te de harae-mass ka?

check (*bill*) okanjō; **could I have the check please?** okanjō, onegai-shi-mass

checkbook kogit-te-chō

checked (*shirt*) chek-ku moyō (no)

checkers chek-kā

check-in chek-ku in

checkroom (*for coats etc*) keitaihin' azukarisho

cheek (*on face*) hō; **what a cheek!** nante atskamashī!

cheeky (*person*) atskamashī

cheerio (*bye-bye*) bai-bai

cheers (*toast*) kampai; (*thank you*) arigatō

cheer up! genki o dashte!

cheese chīz

cheesecake chīzkēki

chef kok-k

chemist (*shop*) ksuri-ya

cheque kogit-te; **will you take a cheque?** kogit-te de harae-mass ka?

cheque book kogit-te-chō

cherry sakurambō

cherry blossom sakura

cherry tree sakura no ki

chess (*Western*) chess; (*Japanese*) shōgi

chest (*of body*) mune

chestnut kuri

chewing gum chūin-gam

chicken niwatori; (*food*) chikin

chickenpox mizubōsō

child kodomo

children kodomotachi

children's playground yūenchi

children's pool kodomo-yō pūru

children's room kodomo-beya

chilled (*wine*) hiyashta; **it's not properly chilled** mada kanzen ni hiete i-masen

chilly samui

chimney entots

chin ago

china setomono

China Chūgok

Chinese (*adjective*) Chūgok (no); (*person*) Chūgok-jin; (*language*) Chūgoku-go; **the Chinese** Chūgok-jin

chips hurenchi-hurai; **potato chips** poteto-chip-p

chocolate chokorēto; **a chocolate bar** itachoko; **a box of chocolates** hakoiri chokorēto; **a hot chocolate** atsui kokoa

choke (*on car*) chōk
choose: it's hard to choose erabu no wa muzukashī dess; **you choose for us** anata ga erande kudasai
chopstick rest hashi-oki
chopsticks hashi
Christmas kurismass; **merry Christmas** merī kurismass
chrysanthemum kik
church kyōkai; **where is the Protestant/Catholic church?** Purotestanto no/Katorik-k no kyōkai wa doko ni ari-mass ka?
cicada semi
cider rin-goshu; *Japanese 'saidā' means lemonade*
cigar hamaki
cigarette tabako; **tipped/plain cigarettes** firutā-tski/firutā-nashi no tabako
cigarette lighter raitā
cine-camera satsueiki
cinema eiga-kan
citizen: I'm a British/American citizen watashi wa Eikok no/Amerika no shimin dess
city toshi
city centre, city center chūshin-gai
claim (*noun: insurance*) baishō yōkyū
claim form baishō yōkyūsho
clarify akiraka ni suru
classical koten (no)
clean (*adjective*) kirei (na); **it's not clean** kirei ja ari-masen; **may I have some clean sheets?** atarashī shītsu o kure-masen ka?; **our apartment hasn't been cleaned today** watashtachi no apāto wa mada sōji shte ari-masen; **can you clean this for me?** kirei ni shte kure-masen ka?
cleaning solution (*for contact lenses*) kontakto-renz-yō kurīnā
cleansing cream (*cosmetic*) kurenjinggu kurīm
clear: it's not very clear hak-kiri shimasen; **ok, that's clear** hai, chanto wakari-mass
clever kashkoi
cliff gake
climate kikō
climb: it's a long climb to the top noboru no ni nagaku kakari-mass;

we're going to climb watashtachi wa noboru tsmori dess
climber tozan-sha
clinic kurinik-k
cloakroom (*for coats*) keitaihin'azukarisho; (*WC*) otearai
clock tokei
clogs geta
close: is it close? chikai dess ka?; **close to the hotel** hoteru ni chikai; **close by** chikai
close: when do you close? its shimemass ka?
closed (*door*) shimat-ta; (*shop*) kyūgyō; **they were closed** (*shops*) kyūgyō deshta
closet oshīre
cloth (*material*) nunoji; (*rag*) zōkin
clothes (*Western*) yōhuk; (*Japanese*) wahuk
clothes line mono-hoshi-tsuna
clothes peg, clothespin sentaku-basami
clouds kumo; **it's clouding over** kumot-te ki-mashta
cloudy kumori (no)
club kurab
clubhouse kurab-kaikan
clumsy bukiyō (na)
clutch (*car*) kurach-chi; **the clutch is slipping** kurach-chi wa suberi-mass
coach (*long distance bus*) chōkyori bass
coach party kashkiri-bass no dantai-kyak
coach trip bass ryokō
coast kaigan; **at the coast** kaigan de
coastguard en-gan-keibitai
coat (*overcoat etc*) kōto; (*jacket*) jaket-to
coathanger han-gā
cobbler kutsunaoshi
cockroach gokiburi
cocktail kakteru
cocktail bar kakteru bā
cocoa kokoa
coconut kokonats
code: what's the (dialling) code for ...? ... no shigai-kyokuban wa namban dess ka?
coffee kōhī; **a white coffee, a coffee with milk** miruku-iri no kōhī; **a black coffee** burak-ku kōhī; **two coffees, please** kōhī hutats, onegaishi-mass

coin: 100-yen coin hyaku-en-dama
Coke (*tm*) Kōk
cold (*thing*) tsmetai; (*weather*) samui;
I'm cold samui dess; **I have a cold**
kaze o hiki-mashta
cold cream (*cosmetic*) kōrudo kurīm
collapse: he's collapsed kare wa
taore-mashta
collar eri
collar bone sakots
colleague: my colleague watashi
no dōryō; **your colleague** anata no
dōryō
collect: I've come to collect ... ... o
uketori ni ki-mashta; **I collect ...**
(*stamps etc*) watashi wa ... o atsumete
i-mass; **I want to call New York
collect** ryōkin sempō-barai de Nyū-
Yōk ni denwa o shtai dess
collect call ryōkin sempō-barai no
denwa
college daigak
collision shōtots
cologne ōdekoron
colo(u)r iro; **do you have any other
colo(u)rs?** bets no iro ga ari-mass
ka?
colo(u)r film karā firum
comb (*noun*) kushi
come kuru; **I come from London**
Rondon shush-shin dess; **where do
you come from?** doko no shush-shin
dess ka?; **when are they coming?**
karera wa its ki-mass ka?; **come here**
koko ni kite kudasai; **come with me**
ish-sho ni kite kudasai; **come back!**
modot-te kudasai; **I'll come back
later** ato de ki-mass; **come in!** (*when
someone knocks at door*) dōzo; (*to guest*)
ohairi kudasai; **he's coming on very
well** (*improving*) kare wa totemo yok
nat-te ki-mashta; **come on!** hayak!;
**do you want to come out this eve-
ning?** kon'ya dete ki-masen ka?;
**these two pictures didn't come out
very well** kono shashin ni-mai wa
yoku utsuranakat-tan dess; **the
money hasn't come through yet**
okane wa mada kite i-masen
comfortable (*hotel etc*) yut-tari shte
iru; **it's not very comfortable** chot-
to yut-tari shte i-masen
comic book man-ga

commemorative kinen; **commemorative stamp** kinen-kit-te
Common Market Ōshū shijō
company (*firm*) kaisha
comparison: there's no comparison
hikak ni nari-masen
compartment (*on train*) kyak-shits
compass rashimban
compensation son-gai-baishō
complain kujō o iu; **I want to
complain about my room** watashi no
heya no koto de kujō ga ari-mass
complaint kujō; **I have a complaint**
kujō ga ari-mass
complete: the complete set kanzen-
na set-to; **it's a complete disaster**
mat-tak no sainan dess
completely kanzen ni
complicated: it's very complicated
hijō ni hukuzats dess
comprehensive (*insurance*) sōgō (no)
computer kompyūtā
concern: we are very concerned
watashtachi wa totemo shimpai shte
i-mass
concert konsāto
concussion nō-shintō
condenser (*in car*) kondensā
**condition: it's not in very good con-
dition** jōkyō wa amari yoku ari-
masen; (*of contract*) jōken
conditioner (*for hair*) rinss
condom kondōm
conductor (*on train*) shashō
conference kaigi
**confirm: can you confirm the res-
ervation?** yoyaku o kakunin shte
kure-masen ka?
confuse: it's very confusing wakari-
nikui dess
congratulations! omedetō!
conjunctivitis ketsmakuen
connection (*in travelling*) renrak
connoisseur kurōto
conscious (*medically*) ishki ga aru
**consciousness: he's lost conscious-
ness** ishki o ushinai-mashta
constipation bempi
consul ryōji
consulate ryōjikan
contact: how can I contact ...? ... ni
dō renrak deki-mass ka?; **I'm trying
to contact ... ...** ni renraku o torō to

shte i-mass
contact lenses kontakto renz
contract keiyak
contraceptive (*pill*) hinin'yak; (*device*)
hinin'yōgu
convenient (*time, location*) tsugō no ī;
that's not convenient sore wa tsugō
ga yoku ari-masen
cook: it's not properly cooked (*is
underdone*) chanto ryōri dekite i-
masen; **it's beautifully cooked**
totemo jōz ni ryōri dekite i-mass;
he's a good cook kare wa ryōri ga
jōz dess
cooker renji
cookie kuk-kī
cool (*day, weather*) suzushī
corduroy kōruten
cork (*in bottle*) koruk-sen
corkscrew koruk-nuki
cormorant fishing ukai
corn (*on foot*) uo no me
corner: on the corner (*of street*)
machikado ni; **in the corner** sumi
ni; **a corner table** sumi no tēburu
cornflakes kōn-hurēk
coronary (*noun*) kanjō dōmyak
correct (*adjective*) tadashī; **please
correct me if I make a mistake**
machigaetara naoshte kudasai
corridor rōka
corset koruset-to
cosmetics keshō-hin
cost: what does it cost? ikura dess
ka?
cot (*for baby*) bebī bed-do
cottage koya
cotton momen
cotton buds (*for make up removal etc*)
membō
cotton wool dash-shimen
couch ne-iss
couchette kyakshits no shindai
cough (*noun*) seki
cough tablets sekidome dorop-p
cough medicine sekidome
could: could you do it? shte kure-
masen ka?; **could I have ...?** ... o
kure-masen ka?; **I couldn't ... ...**
koto wa deki-masen deshta
country (*nation*) kuni; **in the country**
(*countryside*) inaka ni
countryside inaka

couple (*man and woman*) hūhu; **a
couple of ... ...** hutats
courier gaido
course: a five-course dinner go-kōss
no ryōri; **of course** mochiron; **of
course not** mochiron chigai-mass
court (*law*) saibansho; (*tennis*) teniss
kōto
courtesy bus (*airport to hotel etc*)
sōgeisha
cousin itoko; **my cousin** watashi no
itoko
cover charge sābiss-ryō
cow ushi
crab kani
cracked: it's cracked (*plate etc*) sore
wa hibi ga hait-te i-mass
cracker (*biscuit*) kurak-kā
craftshop min-geihin-ten
cramp (*in leg etc*) keiren
crane (*bird*) tsuru
crash: there's been a crash shōtots ga
ari-mashta
crash course (*for learning language
etc*) shūchū kōza
crash helmet herumet-to
crawl (*swimming*) kurōru
crazy nek-kyō-teki (na)
cream (*on milk, in cake, for face*) kurīm
creche (*for babies*) takujisho
credit card kurejit-to kādo
crib (*baby's cot*) bebī bed-do
crisis kiki
crisps poteto-chip-p
crockery tōkirui
crook: he's a crook kare wa sagishi
dess
crossing (*by sea*) ōdan
crossroads jūjiro
crosswalk ōdan hodō
crows hitogomi
crowded (*streets, bars*) konda
crown (*on tooth*) shkan
crucial: it's absolutely crucial mat-
taku ket-tei-teki dess
cruise (*by ship*) kōkai
crutch (*of body*) mata
crutches matsbazue
cry nak; **don't cry** naka-naide
cucumber kyūri
cuisine ryōri
cultural bunka-teki (na)
culture bunka; **cultured pearls**

yōshok-shinju
cup kap-p; **a cup of coffee** kōhī ippai
cupboard oshīre; (*with shelves*) todana
cure: have you got something to cure it? nani ka kore ni kiku mono ga ari-mass ka?
curlers kārā
current (*electrical*) denryū; (*in water*) kairyū
curry karē
curtains kāten
curve (*noun: in road*) kāb
cushion kush-shon; (*for sitting on floor*) zabuton
custom shūkan
Customs zeikan
cut: I've cut my finger yubi o kit-te

shimai-mashta; **could you cut a little off here?** koko o skoshi kit-te kuremasen ka?; **we were cut off** (*telephone*) denwa ga kirete shimaimashta; **the engine keeps cutting out** enjin ga shot-chū tomat-te shimai-mass
cutlery naihu-rui
cutlets katsurets
cycle: can we cycle there? (*is it far?*) soko e jitensha de ike-mass ka?
cyclist saikuristo
cylinder (*of car*) shirindā
cylinder-head gasket shirindā-heddo no gasket-to
cynical hinik (na)
cystitis bōkōen

D

damage: you've damaged it kowaremashta; **it's damaged** kowarete i-mass; **there's no damage** son-gai wa ari-masen
damn! ima-imashī!
damp (*adjective*) shimet-ta
dance: a folk dance fōk-danss; **do you want to dance?** dansu o shimasen ka?
dancer: he's a good dancer kare wa danss ga jōz dess ne
dancing: we'd like to go dancing watashtachi wa danss ni iki-tai dess; **traditional Japanese dancing** kotem-buyō
dandruff huke
dangerous abunai
dare: I don't dare to eat live fish iki-zukuri o taberu yūki wa ari-masen
dark (*adjective*) kurai; **dark blue** kon'iro; **when does it get dark?** its goro kurak nari-mass ka?; **after dark** kurak nat-te kara
dashboard keikiban
date: what's the date? nan-nichi dess ka?; **on what date?** nan-nichi?; **can**

we make a date? (*romantic*) dēto o shi-masen ka?; (*to business partner*) its ga ī dess ka?
dates (*to eat*) natsmeyashi no mi
daughter ojō-san; **my daughter** musume
daughter-in-law giri no musume-san; **my daughter-in-law** giri no musume
dawn (*noun*) yoake; **at dawn** yoake ni
day hi; **the day after** sono tsugi no hi; **the day before** sono mae no hi; **every day** mainichi; **one day** (*once*) aru hi; (*length of time*) ichi-nichi; **can we pay by the day?** higime de harae-mass ka?; **have a good day!** gokigen'yō!
daylight robbery (*extortionate prices*) hōgai na ryōkin
day trip higaeri ryokō
dead shinda
deaf mimi ga tōi
deaf-aid hochōki
deal (*business*) torihiki; **it's a deal** sore de kimari-mashta; **will you deal with it?** sore o yat-te kure-masen ka?

dealer (*agent*) dīrā
dear (*expensive*) takai
death shi
decadent taihai-teki (na)
December jūni-gats
decent: that's very decent of you
sore wa goshinsets-sama
decide: we haven't decided yet
mada kimete i-masen; **you decide
for us** anata ga kimete kudasai;
it's all decided mō sore wa kimat-te
i-mass
decision ket-tei
deck (*on ship*) dek-ki
deckchair dek-ki-cheya
declare: I have nothing to declare
shinkok suru mono wa ari-masen
decoration (*in room*) naisō
deduct sashihik
deep hukai; **is it deep?** hukai dess
ka?
deep-freeze (*noun*) reitō
deer shka
definitely mat-tak sono tōri dess;
definitely not mat-tak chigai-mass
degree (*university*) gakui; (*temperature*)
40 degrees Fahrenheit kashi yonjū-
do; **40 degrees Celsius** sesh-shi
yonjū-do
dehydrated (*person*) dass-sui shōjō
delay: the flight was delayed hikōki
ga okure-mashta
deliberately waza to
delicacy: a local delicacy meibuts
delicious totemo oishī
deliver: will you deliver it? haitats
shte kure-masen ka?
**delivery: is there another mail
delivery?** yūbin no haitats ga mō
ik-kai ari-mass ka?
de luxe gōka (na)
denim (*fabric*) denim
denims jīnz
Denmark Dem-māk
dent: there's a dent in it sore wa
hekonde i-mass
dental floss ha no gomi o toru ito
dentist ha-isha
dentures ireba
deny: he denies it kare wa sore o
hitei shi-mass
deodorant deodoranto
department store depāto

departure shup-pats
departure lounge shup-pats raunji
depend: it depends bāi ni yori-mass;
it depends on ... ... ni yori-mass
deposit (*downpayment*) atamakin
depressed yū-uts (na)
depth hukasa
description setsmei
deserted (*beach, area*) hito-ke no nai
dessert dezāto
destination mokteki-chi
detergent senzai
detour tōmawari
devalued (*currency*) yasku nat-ta
**develop: could you develop these
films?** kono firumu o genzō shte
kure-masen ka?
diabetic (*noun*) tōnyōbyō-kanja
diagram zuhyō
dialect hōgen
dialling code shigai-kyokuban
diamond (*jewel*) daiyamondo
diaper omuts
diarrhoea, diarrhea geri; **do you
have something to stop diarrhoea?**
geri-dome no ksuri ga ari-mass ka?
diary (*planner*) techō; (*for personal
experiences*) nik-ki
dictionary jisho; **a Japanese/English
dictionary** wa-ei jiten
didn't *see* **not** *and page 107*
die shinu; **I'm absolutely dying for a
drink** nodo ga kawaite shini-sō dess
diesel (*fuel*) dīzeru
diet daiet-to; **I'm on a diet** daiet-to-
chū dess
Diet (*Parliament*) Kok-kai
difference chigai; **what's the difference between ...?** ... no chigai wa
nan dess ka?; **I can't tell the difference** sono chigai wa wakari-masen;
it doesn't make any difference
(*choosing between two things*) dot-chi
demo ī dess
different: they are different sorera
wa chigai-mass; **they are very different** sorera wa totemo chigai-mass;
it's different from this one kore to
chigai-mass; **may we have a different table?** chigau tēburu ni shte
kure-masen ka?; **ah well, that's
different** demo sore wa bets dess
difficult muzukashī

difficulty kon-nan; **without any difficulty** kantan ni; **I'm having difficulties with ... ...** ni komat-te i-mass

digestion shōka

dining car shokudōsha

dining room shokudō

dinner yūshok

dinner jacket takshīdo

dinner party bansankai

direct *(adjective)* choksets (no); **does it go direct?** chok-kō shi-mass ka?

direction hōkō; **in which direction is it?** dot-chi no hōkō dess ka?; **is it in this direction?** kono hōkō dess ka?

directory: telephone directory denwa-chō

directory enquiries denwa ban-gō an-nai

dirt yogore

dirty kitanai

disabled shintai shōgai-sha

disappear nakunaru; **it's just disappeared** *(is lost)* nakunat-te shimai-mashta

disappointed: I was disappointed gak-kari shi-mashta

disappointing kitai-hazure (no)

disaster saigai

discharge *(pus)* umi

disc jockey disk jok-kī

disco disko

disco dancing disko danss

discount *(noun)* waribiki

disease byōki

disgusting *(taste, food etc)* iya (na)

dish *(meal)* ryōri; *(plate)* osara

dishcloth hukin

dishwashing liquid shok-ki-yō senzai

disinfectant *(noun)* shōdokzai

disk of film disk firum

dislocated shoulder dak-kyū shta kata

dispensing chemist yak-kyok

disposable nappies kami omuts

distance kyori; **what's the distance from ... to ...?** ... kara ... made dono kurai kyori ga ari-mass ka?; **in the distance** tōk ni

distilled water jōryūsui

distributor *(in car)* haidenki

disturb: the disco is disturbing us disko ga urusai dess

diversion *(traffic)* mawari-michi

diving board tobikomi-dai

divorced rikonshta

dizzy: I feel dizzy memai ga shi-mass; **I get dizzy spells** tokidoki memai ga shi-mass

do suru; **what shall I do?** dō shi-mashō?; **what are you doing tonight?** kon'ya nani o shi-mass ka?; **how do you do?** hajimemashte, dōzo yoroshku; **how do you do it?** dono yō ni shi-mass ka?; **will you do it for me?** shte kure-masen ka?; **who did it?** dare ga shi-mashta ka?; **the meat's not done** nik wa mada dekite i-masen; **what do you do?** *(job)* oshigoto wa nan dess ka?; **do you have ...?** ... ga ari-mass ka?

docks dok-k

doctor oisha-san; **he needs a doctor** oisha-san ga iri-mass; **can you call a doctor?** oisha-san' o yonde kure-masen ka?

document shorui

dog inu

doll nin-gyō

Doll's Festival *(March 3rd)* hina matsuri

dollar doru

donkey roba

don't! dame!; *see* **not** *and pages 107-108*

door doa

doorman doabōi

doorway genkan

dosage tōyakuryō

double: double room daburu; **double bed** daburu bed-do; **double brandy** daburu burandē; **double r** *(in spelling name)* āru hutats; **it's all double Dutch to me** watashi ni wa chimpun-kampun dess

doubt: I doubt it utagawashī to omoi-mass

douche *(medical)* kansui

doughnut dōnats

down: get down! orinasai!; **he's not down yet** *(is in room, bed)* mada orite ki-masen; **further down the road** michi no mot-to saki ni; **I paid 20% down** atamakin ni-wari o harai-mashta

downmarket *(hotel etc)* yasup-poi

downtown Tokyo Tōkyō no shtamachi

downstairs shta

dozen ichi-dāss (no); **half a dozen** han-dāss (no)

drain (*in sink, street*) haisui

draught beer nama-bīru

draughts (*game*) chek-kā

draughty: it's rather draughty skimakaze ga hairi-mass

drawing pin oshi pin

dreadful (*food, holiday, weather etc*) hidoi

dream (*noun*) yume; **it's like a bad dream** (*this trip etc*) akumu no yō dess; **sweet dreams** oyasumi nasai

dress (*woman's*) doress; **I'll just get dressed** chot-to shtaku o shi-mass

dressing (*for wound*) hōtai; (*for salad*) doresh-shing-g

dressing gown gaun

drink (*verb*) nomu; **can I get you a drink?** nomimono wa ikaga dess ka?; **I don't drink** (*alcohol*) arukōru wa nomi-masen; **I must have something to drink** (*alcoholic and non-alcoholic*) nanika nomi-tai dess; **may I have a drink of water?** omizu o itadake-mass ka?; **drink up!** nonde shimai-nasai!; **I had too much to drink** nomi-sugi-mashta

drinkable: is the water drinkable? mizu wa nome-mass ka?

drive: we drove here kuruma de ki-mashta; **I'll drive you home** okut-te iki-mass; **do you want to come for a drive?** doraibu shi-masen ka?; **is it a very long drive?** kuruma demo tōi dess ka?

driver (*of car, bus*) unten-shu

driver's license untem-menkyoshō

driving licence untem-menkyoshō

drizzle: it's drizzling konuka ame ga hut-te i-mass

drop: just a drop (*of drink*) hon no skoshi; **I dropped it** otoshi-mashta; (*gave up*) yame-mashta; **drop in some time** itska yot-te kudasai

drown: he's drowning kare wa oborete i-mass

drugs (*medical*) ksuri; (*narcotic*) mayak

drugstore yak-kyok

drunk (*adjective*) yop-parai (no)

drunken driving inshu unten

dry (*adjective*) kawaita

dry-clean: can I get these dry-cleaned? dorai-kurīning-g shte morae-mass ka?

dry-cleaner dorai-kurīning-gu-ya

duck ahiru

due: when is the bus due? bass wa its kuru haz dess ka?

dumb (*can't speak*) oshi (no); (*stupid*) baka (na)

dummy (*for baby*) oshaburi

durex (*tm*) kondōm

during: during ... ... no aida ni

dust hokori

dustbin gomibako

duty-free (*goods*) menzei

dwarf trees bonsai

dynamo dainamo

dynasty ōchō

dysentery sekiri

E

each: each of them sorezore; **one for each of us** min-na ni hitots-zuts; **how much are they each?** hitotsu ikura dess ka?; **each time ... ...** toki wa itsmo; **we know each other** otagai ni shit-te i-mass

ear mimi

earache: I have earache mimi ga itami-mass

early hayai; **early in the morning** asa hayak; **it's too early** haya-sugi-mass; **a day earlier** ichi-nichi hayak; **half an hour earlier** han-jikan hayak; **I need an early night** hayak

nenakereba nari-masen
early riser: I'm an early riser
watashi wa haya-oki dess
earring iyaring-g
earth (*soil*) tsuchi
earthquake jishin
earthenware tōki
earwig hasami-mushi
east higashi; **to the east** higashi e
Easter huk-kats-sai
easy yasashī; **easy with the cream!**
kurīmu wa son-na ni taksan' iri-masen
eat taberu; **something to eat** nanika
taberumono; **we've already eaten**
watashtachi wa mō tabe-mashta
eau-de-Cologne ōdekoron
eccentric henjin
economic keizai
edible taberareru
education kyōik
eel unagi
efficient (*hotel, organization*) sābiss no ī
egg tamago
eggplant nass
Eire Airurando Kyōwakok
either: either ... or ... ... ka ... ka; I
don't like either of them dochira
mo ski ja ari-masen
elastic (*noun*) gomu-himo
elastic band wagom
Elastoplast (*tm*) bansōkō
elbow hiji
electric denki (no)
electric blanket denki mōhu
electric fire denki hītā
electrician denki-ya-san
electricity denki
electric outlet konsento
electronic denshi
electronics erektoroniks
elegant jōhin (na)
elevator erebētā
else: something else nani ka hoka
no mono; **somewhere else** doko ka
hoka no tokoro; **let's go somewhere**
else doko ka hoka no tokoro e iki-
mashō; **what else?** hoka ni wa?;
nothing else, thanks mō ī dess,
arigatō
embarrassed: he's embarrassed kare
wa haji o kaki-mashta
embarrassing hazkashī

embassy taishkan
emergency hijō; **this is an**
emergency kinkyū dess
emery board tsmeyasuri
emotional (*person, time*) kanjō-teki (na)
Emperor of Japan Ten-nō Heika
Empress of Japan Kōgō Heika
empty kara (no)
end (*noun*) owari; **at the end of the**
road michi no owari ni; **when does**
it end? itsu owari-mass ka?
energetic (*person*) genki (na)
energy: he doesn't have the energy
to do it kare wa sore o suru genki
ga ari-masen
engaged (*to be married*) kon'yakshta;
(*toilet*) shiyō-chū; (*telephone*) hanash-
chū
engagement ring kon'yak yubiwa
engine enjin
engine trouble enjin no koshō
England Igiriss
English (*adjective*) Igiriss (no);
(*language*) Eigo; **the English** Igiriss-
jin; **I'm English** watashi wa Igiriss-
jin dess; **do you speak English?**
Eigo o hanashi-mass ka?
Englishman Igiriss-jin
Englishwoman Igiriss-jin
enjoy: I enjoyed it very much
totemo tanoshkat-ta dess; **enjoy**
yourself! tanoshinde kudasai!
enjoyable tanoshī
enlargement (*of photo*) hikinobashi
enormous totemo ōkī
enough jūbun; **there's not enough**
tari-masen; **it's not big enough** chīsa-sugi-mass; **thank you, that's**
enough arigatō, sore de jūbun dess
entertainment gorak
enthusiastic nesh-shin (na)
entrance (*noun*) iriguchi; (*to house*)
genkan
envelope hūtō
epileptic tenkan (no)
equipment (*in apartment, office, factory*
etc) setsbi
era jidai
eraser keshigom
erotic erochik-k (na)
error machigai
escalator eskarētā
especially tok ni

espresso coffee espuress-so kōhī
essential: it is essential that ... ...
koto wa hitsyō dess
estate agent hudōsan'ya
ethnic (*restaurant*, *clothes*) gaikok-hū
(no); (*problem*) jinshu mondai
Europe Yōrop-pa
European Yōrop-pa-jin
European plan chōshok to yūshok
tski
even: even the English Igiriss-jin
demo; **even if ...** moshi ... demo
evening yūgata; **good evening**
komban wa; **this evening** komban;
in the evening yoru ni; **evening
meal** yūshok
evening dress (*for man*) yakaihuk;
(*for woman*) ibuning-g doress
eventually tsui ni
ever: have you ever been to ...? ... e
it-ta koto ga ari-mass ka?; **if you
ever come to Britain** moshi Eikok ni
irash-shareba
every subete no; **every day** mainichi
everyone min-na
everything subete
everywhere doko demo
exactly! sono tōri dess!
exam shken
example rei; **for example** tatoeba
excellent (*food*, *hotel*) subarashī;
excellent! subarashī!
except igai; **except Sunday** nichiyōbi
igai
exception reigai; **as an exception**
reigai toshte
excess baggage chōka tenimots
excessive kyoktan (na); **isn't that a
bit excessive?** sore wa chot-to iki-
sugi ja ari-masen ka?
exchange (*verb: money*) ryōgae suru;
in exchange kōkan ni
**exchange rate: what's the exchange
rate?** kawase rēto wa ikura dess ka?
exchange student kōkan gaksei
exciting (*day*, *holiday*, *film*) omoshiroi
exclusive (*club*, *hotel*) kōkyū (na)
excursion ensok; **is there an excursion to ...?** ... e ensok shi-masen ka?

excuse me (*to get past*) shitsrei shi-
mass; (*to get attention*) chot-to sumi-
masen; (*pardon?*) e, nan dess ka?
exhaust (*on car*) haiki-kan
exhausted (*tired*) gut-tari
exhibition tenrankai
exist: does it still exist? mada ari-
mass ka?
exit deguchi
expect: I expect so sō deshō; **she's
expecting** kanojo wa ninshin-chū
dess
expensive takai
experience keiken; **an absolutely un-
forgettable experience** totemo
wasurerarenai keiken
experienced keiken no aru
expert (*at martial arts*) tats-jin; (*in electronics etc*) sem-mon-ka
expire: it's expired (*passport etc*)
kigen ga kire-te i-mass
explain setsmei suru; **would you
explain that to me?** sore o setsmei
shte kure-masen ka?
explore tanken suru; **I just want to
go and explore** chot-to tanken shtai
to omoi-mass
export (*verb*) yushuts suru
exports (*noun*) yushuts
exposure meter roshutskei
express (*mail*) soktats; (*train*) tok-kyū
extra: can we have an extra chair?
isu o mō hitots morae-mass ka?; **is
that extra?** (*in cost*) sore wa tsuika-
kin dess ka?
**extraordinarily: extraordinarily
beautiful** totemo kirei (na)
extraordinary (*very strange*) ijō (na)
extremely totemo
extrovert gaikō-teki (na)
**eye me; will you keep an eye on my
bags for me?** chot-to bag-gu o mite
ite kure-masen ka?
eyebrow mayu
eyebrow pencil mayuzumi
eye drops megusuri
eyeliner ai-rainā
eye shadow ai-shadō
eye witness mokugeki-sha

F

fabric nunoji; **silk fabric** kinu orimono
fabulous subarashī
face kao
face mask (*for diving*) mask; (*for colds*) mask
face pack (*cosmetic*) pak-k
facing: facing the sea umi ni menshta
fact jijits
factory kōjō
Fahrenheit kashi; *see page 121*
faint: she's fainted kanojo wa kizets shi-mashta; **I'm going to faint** ki ga tōk nari-sō dess
fair (*fun-fair*) yūenchi; (*commercial*) tenjikai; **that's not fair** hukōhei dess; **OK, fair enough** ja ī dess
fake nise (no)
fall: he's had a fall kare wa korobi-mashta; **he fell off his bike** kare wa jitensha kara ochi-mashta; **in the fall** aki ni
false (*not true*) uso (no); (*not real*) nise (no); (*artificial*) jinkō (no)
false teeth ireba
family kazok
family Buddhist altar butsdan
family name myōji
famished: I'm famished onaka ga peko-peko dess
famous yūmei (na)
fan (*mechanical*) sempūki; (*folding*) ōgi; (*round*) uchiwa; (*football etc*) fan
fan belt famberuto
fancy: he fancies you kare wa anata ga ski dess
fancy dress party kasō pātī
fantastic subarashī
far tōi; **is it far?** tōi dess ka?; **how far is it to ...?** ... wa dono kurai tōi dess ka?; **as far as I'm concerned** watashi no kan-gae de wa
fare ryōkin; **what's the fare to ...?** ...

made ikura dess ka?
fare box (*on buses*) ryōkim-bako
farewell party sōbetskai
farm nōjō
farther mot-to tōk; **farther than ... ...** yori tōi
fashion (*in clothes etc*) ryūkō
fashionable ryūkō (no)
fast hayai; **not so fast** son-na ni hayaku ari-masen; (*just a minute*) chot-to mat-te
fastener (*on clothes*) fasnā
fat (*person*) hutot-ta; (*on meat*) abura
father otō-san; **my father** chichi
father-in-law giri no otō-san; **my father-in-law** giri no chichi
fattening hutori-sō (na)
faucet jaguchi
fault (*defect*) ara; **it was my fault** watashi no sei deshta; **it's not my fault** watashi no sei ja ari-masen
faulty (*equipment*) chōshi ga okashī
favo(u)rite ichi-ban ski (na); **that's my favo(u)rite book** sore wa watashi no ichi-ban ski na hon dess
fawn (*colour*) kyarameru iro
February ni-gats
fed up: I'm fed up unzari shi-mashta; **I'm fed up with ... ...** ni unzari shi-mashta
feeding bottle honyū bin
feel: I feel hot/cold atsui/samui dess; **I feel like a drink** nani ka nomitai to omoi-mass; **I don't feel like it** ki ga mùki-masen; **how are you feeling today?** kyō wa ikaga dess ka?; **I'm feeling a lot better** daibu ī dess; **I don't feel like drinking** nomu ki ni nare-masen
felt-tip (pen) feruto pen
fence hei
fencing kendō
fender (*of car*) doroyoke
ferry ferī; **what time's the last ferry?**

saishū no ferī wa nan-ji dess ka?
festival matsuri
fetch: I'll go and fetch it it-te tot-te
ki-mass; **will you come and fetch
me?** mukae ni kite kure-masen ka?
fever nets
feverish: I'm feeling rather feverish
chot-to nets ga ari-mass
few: only a few hon no skoshi; **a few
minutes** nisam-pun; **he's had a good
few (to drink)** taksan nomi-mashta
fiancé kon'yaksha
fiancée kon'yaksha
fiasco: what a fiasco! sanzan dess ne!
field nohara
fifty-fifty gobugobu
fight (*noun*) kenka
figs ichijik
figure (*of person*) taikei; (*number*) sūji;
I have to watch my figure taikei ni
ki o tskenakereba nari-masen
fill ip-pai ni suru; **fill it up please** ip-
pai ni shte kudasai; **fill her up
please** mantan ni shte kudasai; **will
you help me fill out this form?**
kakikata o oshiete kure-masen ka?
fillet (*meat*) hire-nik; (*fish*) katami
filling (*in tooth*) ha no tsmemono; **it's
very filling** (*food*) onaka ga ip-pai ni
nari-mass ne!
filling station gasorin stando
film (*at cinema*) eiga; (*for camera*)
firum; **do you have this type of
film?** kon-na firum ga ari-mass ka?;
16mm film jūroku-miri firum;
35mm film sanjūgo-miri firum
filter (*for camera, coffee*) firutā
filter-tipped firutā-tski
filthy (*room etc*) kitanai
find mitskeru; **I can't find it**
mitskari-masen; **if you find it** moshi
mitsketara; **I've found a ... ...** o
mitske-mashta
fine: it's fine weather ī tenki dess; **a
10,000 yen fine** ichi man'en no bak-
kin; **how are you? — fine thanks**
ogenki dess ka? — okage-sama de
finger yubi
fingernail tsme
finish: I haven't finished owat-te i-
masen; **when I've finished** watashi
ga owat-tara; **when does it finish?**
itsu owari-mass ka?; **finish off your**

drink nonde shimainasai
fire: fire! (*something's on fire*) kaji!; **it's
on fire** kaji dess; **it's not firing
properly** (*car*) umak tenka shte i-
masen
fire alarm kasai hōchki
fire brigade/department shōbōsho
fire escape hijōguchi
fire extinguisher shōkaki
firefly hotaru
fireworks hanabi
firm (*company*) kaisha
first saisho (no); **I was first** watashi ga
ichi-ban deshta; **at first** saisho ni;
this is the first time kore ga
hajimete dess
first aid ōkyū teate
first aid kit kyūkyūbako
first class (*travel etc*) it-tō
fish (*noun*) sakana; (*raw fish prepared*)
sashimi; (*raw fish on rice*) nigiri-zushi
fisherman ryōshi
fishing tsuri
fishing boat gyosen
fishing net ami
fishing rod tsurizao
fishing tackle tsuri-dōgu
fishing village gyoson
fit (*health*) jōbu (na); **I'm not very fit**
amari jōbu ja ari-masen; **he's a keep
fit fanatic** kare wa kīpufit-to ni
nesh-shin dess; **it doesn't fit** sore wa
ai-masen
fix: can you fix it? (*repair*) naose-mass
ka?; **let's fix a time** jikan'o kime-
mashō; **it's all fixed up** mō kimat-te
i-mass; **I'm in a bit of a fix** chot-to
komat-te i-mass
fizzy tansan (no)
fizzy drink tansan' inryō
flab (*on body*) tarumi
flag hata
flannel neru
flash (*for camera*) hurash
flashlight kaichū dentō
flashy (*clothes etc*) kebakebashī
flat (*adjective*) taira (na); **this beer is
flat** kono bīru wa ki ga nukete i-
mass; **I've got a flat tyre/tire** taiya
ga pank shi-mashta; (*apartment*)
apāto
flatterer gomasuri
flatware (*cutlery*) naihu-rui; (*crockery*)

osara-rui
flavo(u)r aji
flexible (*material*) danryok-teki (na);
(*arrangements*) jiyū no kik
flies (*on trousers*) zubon no fasnā
flight hikō-bin
flirt (*verb*) ichatsku
flood kōzui
floor (*of room*) yuka; **on the floor** yuka
ni; **on the second floor** (*UK*) san-gai
ni; (*US*) ni-kai ni
floorshow huroashō
flop (*failure*) ship-pai
florist hana-ya
flour komugiko
flower hana
flower arranging ikebana
flu ryūkan
fluent: he speaks flluent Japanese
kare wa Nihon-go o ryūchō ni
hanashi-mass
fly (*verb*) tobu; **can we fly there?**
hikōki de ike-mass ka?
fly (*insect*) hae
fly spray haetori spurē
foggy: it's foggy kiri ga dete i-mass
fog lights fog-gu raito
folk dancing fōk danss
folk music minzoku on-gak
follow tsuite ik; **follow me** tsuite kite
kudasai
fond: I'm quite fond of ... ... ga ski
dess
food tabemono; **the food's excellent**
tabemono wa subarashī dess
food poisoning shokchūdok
food store shokuryōhin-ten
fool baka
foolish baka (na)
foot ashi; **on foot** aruite; *see page 119*
foot warmer kotats
football (*game*) sak-kā; (*ball*) hut-to-
bōru
for: is that for me? sore wa watashi
no tame ni?; **what's this for?** nan no
tame ni?; **for two days** hutskakan;
I've been here for a week mō ish-
shūkan koko ni i-mass; **a bus for ...**
... iki no bass
forbidden kinjirareta
forehead hitai
foreign gaikok (no)
foreigner gaikok-jin

foreign exchange (*money*) gaikoku-
kawase
forest mori
forget wasureru; **I forget, I've for-
gotten** wasurete shimai-mashta;
don't forget wasurenaide kudasai
fork (*for eating*) hōk; (*in road*) sansaro
form (*in hotel, to fill out*) yōshi
formal (*dress, person, language*)
keishki-teki (na)
fortnight ni-shūkan
fortunately un'yok
fortune-teller uranaishi
**forward: could you forward my
mail?** tegami o tensō shte kure-
masen ka?
forwarding address iten saki
foundation cream fandēshon kurīm
fountain (*ornamental*) hunsui; (*for
drinking*) mizu-nomiba
fox kitsne
foyer (*of hotel, theatre*) robī
fracture (*noun*) koss-sets
fractured skull zugaikots koss-sets
fragile (*thing*) koware-yasui;
(*person*) yowayowashī
frame (*for picture*) gak
France Huranss
fraud (*action*) sagi; (*person*) sagishi
free (*no charge*) tada; (*time*) hima;
admission free nyūjō muryō
freezer reitōko
freezing cold kogoe-sō ni samui
French (*adjective*) Huranss no;
(*language*) Huranss-go
French fries hurench hurai
frequent tabitabi (no)
fresh (*weather, breeze*) sawayaka (na);
(*fruit etc*) shinsen (na); (*cheeky*)
namaiki (na); **don't get fresh with
me** namaiki o iwanaide
fresh orange juice nama no orenji-
jūss
friction tape zetsuen tēp
Friday kin'yōbi
fridge reizōko
fried egg medamayaki
fried rice yakimeshi
friend tomodachi
friendly shtashimi no aru
frog kaeru
from: I'm from London Rondon
shush-shin dess; **from here to the**

sea koko kara umi made; **the next boat from ... ...** kara no tsugi no bōto; **as from Tuesday** kayōbi kara

front mae; **in front** mae ni; **in front of us** watashtachi no mae ni; **at the front** mae ni

frozen reitō shta

frozen food reitō shok-hin

fruit kudamono

fruit juice hurūts jūss

fruit salad hurūts sarada

frustrating: it's very frustrating ira-ira shi-mass

fry ageru; **nothing fried** agemono wa dame dess

frying pan hurai pan

full ip-pai; **it's full of ... ...** de ip-pai dess; **I'm full** (*eating*) onaka ga ip-pai dess

full-board sanshok tski

full-bodied (*wine*) kok no aru

fun: it's fun tanoshī dess; **it was great fun** totemo tanoshkat-ta dess; **just for fun** kibarashi ni; **have fun** tanoshinde kudasai

funeral sōshki

funny (*strange*) okashī; (*amusing*) omoshiroi

furniture kagu

further mot-to tōk; **2 kilometres further** mō ni-kiro mukō; **further down the road** sono michi no mot-to mukō

fuse (*noun*) hyūz; **the lights have fused** denki no hyūz ga kire-mashta

fuse wire hyūz-yō harigane

future shōrai; **in future** kore kara

G

gale ōkaze

gallon see page 121

gallstones tanseki

gamble kakegoto; **I don't gamble** kakegoto wa shi-masen

game gēm

games room gēm rūm

gammon kunsei no ham

gangster yakuza

garage (*petrol*) gasorin stando; (*repair*) shūrikōjō; (*for parking*) shako

garbage gomi

garden niwa

garlic nin-nik

gas gass; (*gasoline*) gasorin

gasket gasket-to

gas pedal akseru

gas permeable lenses tsūki-sei renz

gas station gasorin stando

gas tank gastank

gastroenteritis ichōen

gate mon; (*at airport*) gēto

gauge gēji

gay (*homosexual*) homo (no)

gear giya; **the gears keep sticking** giya ga katak nari-mashta

gearbox giyabok-ks; **I have gearbox trouble** giyabok-ks no chōshi ga yoku ari-masen

gear lever, gear shift giya rebā

geisha (girl) geisha

general delivery kyok-dome

generous: that's very generous of you anata wa totemo kimae ga ī dess

gentleman (*man*) kata; **that gentleman over there** asoko ni iru kata; **he's such a gentleman** kare wa totemo shinshi-teki dess

gents (*toilet*) dansei-yō toire

genuine hom-mono

German Doits (no); (*person*) Doits-jin; (*language*) Doits-go

German measles hūshin

Germany Doits

get: have you got ...? ... ga ari-mass ka?; **how do I get to ...?** ... e dō ikeba ī dess ka?; **where do I get it from?** doko de morae-mass ka?; **can I get you a drink?** nomimono wa ikaga dess ka?; **will you get it for**

me? mot-te kite kure-masen ka?;
when do we get there? its tski-mass
ka?; **I've got to ...** ...-nakereba nari-
masen; **I've got to go** ikanakereba
nari-masen; **where do I get off?**
doko de ori-mass ka?; **it's difficult
to get to** ik no wa muzukashī dess;
when I get up (*in morning*) okiru
toki
ghastly osoroshī
ghost yūrei
giddy: it makes me giddy hurahura
shi-mass
gift okurimono
gigantic kyodai (na)
gin jin; **a gin and tonic** jin-tonik-k
ginko nut gin-nan
girl on-na no ko
girlfriend gāruhurendo
give ageru; **will you give me ...?** ... o
kure-masen ka?; **I'll give you 1000
yen** sen' en' age-mass; **I gave it to
him** sore o kare ni age-mashta; **will
you give it back?** kaeshte kure-
masen ka?; **would you give this to
...?** kore o ... ni agete kure-masen
ka?
glad ureshī
glamorous (*woman*) miryok-teki (na)
gland sen
glandular fever sen-nets
glass (*material*) garass; (*for drinking*)
kop-p; **a glass of water** omizu ip-pai
glasses (*spectacles*) megane
gloves tebukuro
glue (*noun*) nori
gnat buyo
go ik; **we want to got to ...** ... e ikitai
to omoi-mass; **I'm going there
tomorrow** ashta iki-mass; **when does
it go?** (*bus etc*) nan-ji ni de-mass ka?;
where are you going? doko e iki-
mass ka?; **let's go** iki-mashō!; **he's
gone** kare wa it-te shimai-mashta;
it's all gone mō ari-masen; **I went
there yesterday** kinō iki-mashta; **a
hamburger to go** hambāg hitots,
mochi-kaeri; **go away!** at-chi e it-te!;
it's gone off (*milk etc*) kusat-te
shimai-mashta; **we're going out
tonight** kon'ya dekake-mass; **do you
want to go out tonight?** kon'ya
dekaketai to omoi-mass ka?; **has the**

price gone up? nedan ga agari-
mashta ka?
go-between nakōdo
goal (*sport*) gōru
goat yagi
god kami
goddess megami
gold kin
goldfish kin-gyo
golf goruhu
golf clubs goruhu kurab
golf course goruhujō
good ī; **good!** yokat-ta!; **that's no
good** sore wa dame dess!; **good
heavens!** oya-oya!
goodbye sayonara
good-looking kirei (na)
gooey (*food etc*) nebanebashta
gorgeous (*meal*) gōka (na); (*woman*)
karei (na)
gourmet shokudōrak
gourmet food bishok
government seihu
governor: prefectural governor chiji
gradually dandan
graduate (*verb*) sotsgyō suru; (*noun*)
daigak-sots
grammar bumpō
gram(me) guram; *see page 119*
granddaughter omago-san; **my
granddaughter** magomusume
grandfather ojī-san; **my grandfather**
sohu
grandmother obā-san; **my grandmother** sobo
grandson omago-san; **my grandson**
magomusko
grapefruit gurēp-hurūts
grapefruit juice gurēp-hurūts jūss
grapes budō
grass ksa
grateful kansha (no); **I'm very grateful to you** anata ni totemo kansha
shte i-mass
gravy gurēbī
gray hai-iro (no)
grease (*for car*) gurīss; (*on food*) abura
greasy (*food*) aburak-koi
great: a great scholar idai na gaksha;
that's great! subarashī!
Great Britain Eikok
Greece Girisha

greedy (*for food*) kuishimbō (no); (*for things*) yokubari (na)
green midori-iro (no)
green car (*on railway*) gurīn-sha
greengrocer yao-ya
green tea ocha
grey hai-iro (no)
grilled guriru de yaita
gristle (*on meat*) nankots
grocer's shokuryōhin-ten
ground (*land*) tochi; (*sports*) kyōgi-jō; **on the ground** jimen ni; **on the ground floor** ik-kai ni
ground beef ushi no hikinik
group gurūp
group insurance gurūp hoken

group leader gurūp rīdā
guarantee (*noun*) hoshō; **is it guaranteed?** hoshō tski dess ka?
guardian (*of child*) hogosha
guest okyaksan
guesthouse geshkuya
guest room kyakshits
guide (*person*) gaido
guidebook gaido buk-k
guilty yūzai (no)
guitar gitā
gum (*in mouth*) haguki; (*chewing gum*) gam
gun (*rifle*) jū; (*pistol*) pistoru
gymnasium tai-ikukan
gyn(a)ecologist hujinka no oisha-san

H

hair kami
hairbrush burash
haircut (*for men*) sampats; (*for women*) kat-to; **just an ordinary haircut please** hutsū ni onegai-shi-mass
hairdresser biyōin
hairdryer doraiyā
hair grip hea-kurip-p
half hambun; **half an hour** han-jikan; **a half portion** hambun; **half a litre/ liter** han-rit-toru; **half as much** hambun; **half as much again** ichi-bai han; *see page 117*
halfway: halfway to Kyushu Kyūshū e no tochū
ham ham
hamburger hambāg
hammer (*noun*) kanazuchi
hand te; **will you give me a hand?** tetsdat-te kure-masen ka?
handbag handobag-g
hand baggage tenimots
handbrake handoburēki
handkerchief hankachi
handle (*noun*) handoru; **will you handle it?** sore o yat-te kure-masen ka?
hand luggage tenimots

handmade tezukuri (no)
handsome hansam (na)
hanger (*for clothes*) han-gā
hanging scroll kakejik
hangover hutskayoi; **I've got a terrible hangover** waruyoi shimashta
happen okoru; **how did it happen?** dōshte son-na koto ni nari-mashta ka?; **what's happening today?** kyō wa dō shi-mass ka?; **what's happening here?** dō ka shtan dess ka?; **it won't happen again** mō son-na koto wa okoshi-masen
happy ureshī; **we're not happy with the room** heya ni wa manzok dekimasen
harbo(u)r minato
hard katai; (*difficult*) muzukashī
hard-boiled egg katayude tamago
hard lenses hādo renz
hardly hotondo ...-masen; **I hardly ever go** hotondo iki-masen; **I hardly ever have it (to eat)** hotondo tabemasen; **I hardly ever drink** arukōru o hotondo nomi-masen; *see page 110*
hardware store kanamono-ya
harm (*noun*) gai

harmony chōwa

hassle: it's too much hassle mendō-sugi-mass; **we had a hassle-free trip** nanigoto mo nai ryokō deshta

hat bōshi

hate: I hate ... ... ga daikirai dess

have mots; **do you have ...?** ... o mot-te i-mass ka?; **can I have ...?** ... o kure-masen ka?; **can I have some water?** omizu itadake-mass ka?; **I don't have ...** (*things*) ... o mot-te i-masen; **I have ...** (*things*) ... o mot-te i-mass; **I have ...** (*people*) ... ga i-mass; **I have a brother** kyōdai ga hitori i-mass; **can we have breakfast in our room?** heya de chōshok deki-mass ka?; **have another** mō hitots dōzo; **I have to leave early** hayak denakereba nari-masen; **do I/ we have to pay now?** ima harau hitsyō ga ari-mass ka?; *see page 109*

hay fever kahum-byō

he kare; **is he here?** kare wa koko ni i-mass ka?; **where does he live?** kare wa doko ni sunde i-mass ka?; *see page 99*

head atama; **we're heading for Kyoto** Kyōto ni mukat-te i-mass

headache zutsū

headlights hed-do raito

headphones hed-do hōn

head waiter kyūji-chō

head wind mukaikaze

health kenkō; **your health!** kenkō o iwat-te kampai!

healthy (*person, food*) kenkō (na); (*climate*) kenkō ni yoi

hear: can you hear me? kikoe-mass ka?; **I can't hear you** kikoe-masen; **I've heard about it** kīta koto ga ari-mass

hearing aid hochōki

heart (*organ*) shinzō; (*emotion*) kokoro

heart attack shinzō mahi

heat atsusa; **not in this heat!** kono atsusa no naka de?

heater (*in car*) hītā

heating dambō

heat rash asemo

heat stroke nish-shabyō

heatwave nep-pa

heavy omoi

hectic isogashī

heel (*of foot*) kakato; (*of shoe*) hīru; **could you put new heels on these?** hīru o naoshte kure-masen ka?

heelbar kutsunaoshi

height takasa; (*place*) takai tokoro; **what height is it?** takasa wa dore kurai ari-mass ka?; **I am afraid of heights** takai tokoro ga kowai dess

helicopter herikoptā

hell: oh hell! shimat-ta!

hello! (*in morning*) ohayō-gozai-mass; (*in afternoon*) kon-nichiwa; (*in evening*) komban wa; (*in surprise*) ā!; (*on phone*) moshimoshi

helmet (*for motorcycle*) herumet-to

help (*verb*) tetsdau; **can you help me?** tetsdat-te kure-masen ka?; **thanks for your help** dōmo arigatō; **help!** taskete!

helpful: he was very helpful kare ni wa totemo taskari-mashta; **that's helpful** sore wa taskari-mass

helping: one helping (*of food*) ichi-nim-mae; **another helping** okawari

hepatitis kan'en

her kanojo; **I don't know her** kanojo o shiri-masen; **will you send it to her?** kanojo ni okut-te kure-masen ka?; **it's her** kanojo dess; **with her** kanojo to; **it's for her** kanojo no dess; **that's her suitcase** sore wa kanojo no sūtskēss dess; *see pages 100, 113*

herbs (*cooking*) hāb; (*medicine*) yaksō

here koko; **here you are** (*giving something*) hai dōzo; **here he comes** hora, kare ga ki-mashta

hers kanojo no; **that's hers** sore wa kanojo no dess; *see page 101*

hey! chot-to!

hiccups shak-kuri

hide kakureru

hideous (*taste, weather*) iya (na)

hi-fi hai-fai

high takai

highchair kodomo-yō koshkake

highlighter (*cosmetic*) hairaito

highway kōsok dōro

hiking haiking-g

hill oka; **it's further up the hill** oka no mot-to ue ni ari-mass

hillside sampuk

hilly kihuk no ōi

him kare; **I don't know him** kare o
shiri-masen; **will you send it to
him?** kare ni okut-te kure-masen
ka?; **it's him** kare dess; **with him**
kare to; **it's for him** kare no dess;
see page 100
hip oshiri
hire kariru; **can I hire a car?** kuruma
o karirare-mass ka?; **do you hire
them out?** karirare-mass ka?
his: it's his drink kare no nomimono
dess; **it's his** kare no dess; *see pages
101, 113*
history: the history of Japan Nihon
no rekshi
hit naguru; **he hit me** kare ni
nagurare-mashta; **I hit my head**
atama o uchi-mashta
hitch: is there a hitch? mondai dess
ka?
hitch-hike hit-chi haik
hitch-hiker hit-chi haik suru hito
hit record hit-to rekōdo
hole ana
holiday yasumi; **I'm on holiday**
yasumi dess
Holland Oranda
home uchi; **at home** (*in my house etc*)
uchi de; (*in my country*) kuni de; **I go
home tomorrow** ashta uchi ni kaeri-
mass; **home sweet home** itoshī
wagaya
home address jitak no jūsho
homemade tesei (no)
homesick: I'm homesick hōm-shik-k
ni nari-mashta
honest shōjiki (na)
honestly? hontō ni?
honey hachimits
honeymoon shinkon ryokō; **it's our
honeymoon** watashtachi no shinkon
ryokō dess
honeymoon suite shinkom-beya
hood (*of car*) bon-net-to
hoover (*tm*) sōjiki
hope kibō; **I hope so** sō da to ī dess
nē; **I hope not** sō de nai to ī dess nē
horn (*of car*) keiteki
horrible osoroshī
hors d'oeuvre ōdōburu

horse uma
hose (*for car radiator*) hōss
hospital byōin
hospitality motenashi; **thank you for
your hospitality** omotenashi itadaki-
mashte dōmo arigatō gozai-mashta
hostel hosteru
hot atsui; (*curry etc*) karai; **I'm hot**
atsui dess; **something hot to eat**
nanika atatakai tabemono; **it's so hot
today** kyō wa totemo atsui dess ne
hotdog hot-to dog-g
hotel (*Western-style*) hoteru; (*Japanese-
style*) ryokan; **at my hotel** watashi no
hoteru/ryokan de
hotel clerk (*receptionist*) uketske
hot-water bottle yutampo
hour jikan; **on the hour** ichi-jikan'oki
ni
house ie
housewife shuhu
hovercraft hōbākurahuto
how dō; **how many?** ikuts (no)?; **how
much?** (*price*) ikura?; (*amount*) dono
kurai?; **how often?** nando kurai?;
how are you? ogenki dess ka?; **how
do you do?** hajime-mashte; **how
about a beer?** bīru wa ikaga dess
ka?; **how nice!** nante steki!; **would
you show me how to?** dō suru no
ka oshiete kure-masen ka?
humid mushiatsui
humidity shik-ki
**humo(u)r: where's your sense of
humo(u)r?** anata no yūmoa wa doko
e it-ta no?
hundredweight *see page 120*
hungry: I'm hungry onaka ga suite
i-mass; **I'm not hungry** onaka wa
suite i-masen
hurry: I'm in a hurry isoide i-mass;
hurry up! isoide kudasai!; **there's no
hurry** isogu koto wa ari-masen
hurt: it hurts itami-mass; **my back
hurts** senaka ga itami-mass
husband goshujin; **my husband**
shujin; **her husband** kanojo no
goshujin
hydrofoil suichū yoksen
hydrangea ajisai

I

I watashi; **I am English** Igiriss-jin dess; **I live in Manchester** Manchestā ni sunde i-mass; *see page 99*
ice kōri; **with ice** kōri-iri; **with ice and lemon** kōri to remon'iri
ice cream aiss-kurīm
ice-cream cone aiss-kurīm no kōn
iced coffee aiss-kōhī
ice lolly aiss-kyandē
idea kan-gae; **good idea!** ī kan-gae dess!
ideal (*solution, time*) risō-teki (na)
identity papers mimoto shōmeisho
ideograph kanji
idiot hakchi
idyllic bok-ka-teki (na)
if moshi; **if you could** moshi dekireba; **if not** moshi dame nara
ignition tenka-sōchi
ill byōki; **I feel ill** kibun ga suguremasen
illegal hōritsu ihan (no)
illegible yomi-nikui
illness byōki
imitation (*leather etc*) imitēshon
immediately sugu
immigration ijū
Imperial Palace kōkyo
import (*verb*) yunyū suru
imports yunyū
important taisets (na); **it's very important** totemo taisets dess; **it's not important** taisets ja ari-masen
impossible hukanō (na)
impressive inshō-teki (na)
improve: it's improving yok nat-te i-mass; **I want to improve my Japanese** watashi wa Nihon-go ga jōz ni naritai to omoi-mass
improvement kaizen
in: (*with verbs like 'be', 'live' etc*) ... ni; (*with verbs of action*) ... de; **he lives in Japan** kare wa Nihon ni sunde i-

mass; **I bought it in Japan** Nihon de kai-mashta; **in my room** watashi no heya ni/de; **in London** Rondon ni/de; **in one hour's time** ichi-jikan' ato de; **in August** hachi-gats ni; **in English** Eigo de; **in Japanese** Nihon-go de; **is he in?** kare wa i-mass ka?
incense senkō
inch inchi; *see page 119*
include hukumeru; **is that included in the price?** sore mo ryōkin ni hukumarete i-mass ka?
incompetent yak ni tatanai
inconvenient huben (na)
increase (*noun*) zōka
incredible (*very good, amazing*) shinjirarenai
indecent gehin (na)
independent (*adjective*) dokurits (no)
India Indo
Indian (*adjective*) Indo (no); (*person*) Indo-jin
indicator (*on car*) hōkōshijiki
indigestion shōka huryō
indoor pool okunai pūru
indoors okunai
industry san-gyō; (*as opposed to commerce*) kōgyō
inefficient kōrits no warui
infection kansen
infectious densensei (no)
inflammation enshō
inflation inhure
informal (*clothes, occasion, meeting*) keishki-baranai
information jōhō
information desk an-naisho
information office an-naisho
injection chūsha
injured kega o shta; **she's been injured** kanojo wa kega o shi-mashta
injury kega
Inland Sea Setonaikai

in-law giri no shinrui
inn: **Japanese inn** ryokan
innocent mujaki (na); (*in law*) mujits
(no)
inquisitive sensak-zuki (na)
insect mushi
insect bite mush-sasare
insecticide sat-chū zai
insect repellent mushi-yoke
inside: **inside the temple** otera no
naka; **let's sit inside** naka ni suwari-
mashō
insincere humajime (na)
insomnia humin-shō
instant coffee instanto kōhī
instead kawari ni; **I'll have that one
instead** kawari ni sore ni shi-mass;
instead of ... ... no kawari ni
insulating tape zetsuen tēp
insulin inshurin
insult (*noun*) bujok
insurance hoken; **write your
company insurance here** koko ni
kaisha hoken' o kaite kudasai
insurance policy hoken shōken
intellectual (*noun*) chishki-jin
intelligent sōmei (na)
intentional: **it wasn't intentional**
wazato ja ari-masen deshta
interest: **places of interest** kyōmi no
aru tokoro
interested: **I'm very interested in ...
...** ni totemo kyōmi ga ari-mass
interesting omoshiroi; **that's very
interesting** sore wa totemo
omoshiroi dess
international koksai-teki (na)
international driving licence/
license koksai untem menkyo
interpret tsūyak suru; **would you
interpret?** tsūyak shte kure-masen
ka?
interpreter tsūyak
intersection (*crossroads*) kōsaten
interval (*during play etc*) kyūkei jikan
into: **do come into the room** dōzo

heya ni ohairi kudasai; **shall we go
into the lounge?** raunji ni hairi
mashō ka?; **can you translate that
into English?** Eigo ni yakshte kure-
masen ka?; **I'm not into that** (*don't
like*) sore wa ski ja ari-masen
introduce: **may I introduce ...?** ... o
goshōkai shi-mass
introduction shōkai; **letter of introduction** shōkaijō
introvert naikō-teki (na)
invalid (*not valid*) mukō (na); (*not
healthy*) byōnin
invalid chair kuruma-iss
invitation shōtai; **thank you for the
invitation** goshōtai kudasai-mashte
arigatō gozai-mass
invite shōtai suru; **can I invite you
out?** watashi to dekake-masen ka?
involved: **I don't want to get involved in it** sore ni wa kakawari-
taku ari-masen
iodine yōdo
Ireland Airurando
iris (*flower*) (*Japanese*) ayame; (*Western*)
airiss
Irish Airurando (no)
Irishman Airurando-jin
Irishwoman Airurando-jin
iron (*material*) tets; (*for clothes*) airon;
can you iron these for me? airon
shte kure-masen ka?
ironmonger kanamono-ya
is *see pages 108, 111*
island shima
isolated korits shta
it: **is it ...?** ... dess ka?; **where is it?**
doko dess ka?; **it's her** kanojo dess;
it was ... ... deshta; **that's just it** (*just
the problem, it's a nuisance*) sore nan
dess; **that's it** (*that's right*) sono tōri
dess; *see page 100*
Italy Itaria.
itch: **it itches** kayui dess
itinerary ryotei
ivory zōge

J

jack (*for car*) jak-ki
jacket jaket-to
jade hisui
jam jam; **a traffic jam** kōtsū mahi; **I
jammed on the brakes** chikara ip-pai
burēki o kake-mashta
January ichi-gats
Japan Nihon
Japanese (*adjective*) Nihon (no); (*made
in Japan*) Nihonsei (no); (*person*)
Nihon-jin; (*language*) Nihon-go; **the
Japanese** Nihon-jin
Japanese balalaika shamisen
Japanese bedding huton
Japanese chess shōgi
Japanese fencing kendō
Japanese flute shakuhachi
Japanese harp koto
Japanese paper washi
Japanese-style wahū
Japanese-style hotel ryokan
Japanese tea ocha
Japan Sea Nihonkai
jaundice ōdan
jaw ago
jazz jaz
jazz club jaz kurab
jealous shit-to bukai; **he's jealous**
kare wa shit-to shte i-mass
jeans jīnz
jellyfish kurage
jetlag jisa-boke; **I'm/he's suffering
from jetlag** mada jisa-boke dess
jet-set jet-to zok
jetty sambashi
Jew Yudaya-jin
jewel(le)ry hōseki
Jewish Yudaya (no)
jiffy: just a jiffy chot-to mat-te
job shigoto; **just the job!** (*just
right*) masashku!; **it's a good job
you told me!** sore o oshiete kurete
yokat-ta!
jog: I'm going for a jog joging-g ni

it-te ki-mass
jogging joging-g
join: I'd like to join hairi-tai to
omoi-mass; **can I join you!** (*go with*)
ish-sho ni it-te mo ī dess ka?; (*sit
with*) ish-sho ni suwat-te mo ī dess
ka?; **do you want to join us?** (*go
with*) ish-sho ni iki-masen ka?; (*sit
with*) ish-sho ni suwari-masen ka?
joint (*in body*) kansets; (*to smoke*)
marifana tabako
joke jōdan; **you've got to be joking!**
gojōdan deshō!; **it's no joke** jōdan ja
ari-masen'yo
jolly: it was jolly good totemo
yokat-ta dess; **jolly good!** yokat-ta!
joss stick senkō
journey ryokō; **have a good journey!**
dōzo gobuji de!; **safe journey!** dōzo
gobuji de!
judo jūdō
jug mizusashi; **a jug of water**
mizusashi ip-pai no mizu
July shchi-gats
jump: you made me jump bik-kuri
shi-mashta; **jump in!** (*to car*) dōzo
not-te kudasai!
jumper sētā
junction (*station*) renraku-eki; (*road*)
kōsaten; (*motorway*) intāchenji
June roku-gats
junior: Mr Jones junior wakai hō no
Jōnz-san
junk (*rubbish*) kuzu; (*boat*) jank
just: just one hitots dake; **just me**
watashi dake; **just for me** watashi ni
dake; **just a little** hon no skoshi;
just here masa ni koko de; **not just
now** ima wa dame dess; **that's just
right** chōdo ī dess; **it's just as good**
sore dat-te ī dess yo; **he was here
just now** kare wa tat-ta ima koko ni
i-mashta; **I've only just arrived**
chōdo tsuita bakari dess

K

karate karate
keen: I'm not keen ki ga susumi-masen
keep: can I keep it? morat-te ī dess ka?; **please keep it** dōzo omochi kudasai; **keep the change** otsuri wa kek-kō dess; **will it keep?** (*food*) mochi-mass ka?; **it's keeping me awake** nemure-masen; **it keeps on breaking** sugu koware-mass; **I can't keep anything down** (*food*) sugu ni modoshte shimai-mass
kerb huchi ishi
kerosene tōyu
ketchup kechap-p
kettle yakan
key kagi
kid: the kids kodomotachi; **I'm not kidding** jōdan ja ari-masen
kidneys (*in body, food*) jinzō
kill koross; **my feet are killing me** ashi ga itakte shini-sō dess
kilo kiro; *see page 120*
kilometre, kilometer kirōmētoru; *see page 119*
kimono kimono
kind: that's very kind sore wa goshinsets ni; **this kind of ...** kono yō na ...
kiosk baiten
kiss (*noun*) kiss; (*verb*) kiss suru
kitchen daidokoro

kitchenette kan'i daidokoro
kite tako
kite-flying tako-age
Kleenex (*tm*) kurīneks
knee hiza
kneecap hiza no sara
knickers hujin'yō pants
knife naihu
knitting amimono
knitting needles bōbari
knock: there's a knocking noise from the engine enjin ga nok-k shte i-mass; **he's had a knock on the head** kare wa atama o uchi-mashta; **he's been knocked over** kare wa kuruma ni hanerare-mashta
knot (*in rope*) musubime
know (*somebody, something*) shit-te i-mass; **I don't know** shiri-masen; **do you know a good restaurant?** ī restoran' o shit-te i-mass ka?; **who knows!** dare ni mo wakari-masen; **I didn't know that** shiri-masen deshta; **I don't know him** kare o shiri-masen
Korea Kankok; **North Korea** Kita-Chōsen; **South Korea** Minami-Chōsen
Korean (*adjective*) Kankok (no); (*person*) Kankok-jin; (*language*) Kankoku-go; **the Koreans** Kankok-jin

L

label ret-teru
laces (*for shoes*) ktsu-himo
lacquer ware shik-ki
ladies (room) keshōshits
lady hujin; **ladies and gentlemen!** mina-san!
lager rāgā; **lager and lime** rāgā to raim
lake mizu-umi
lamb kohitsuji
lamp stando
lamppost gaitō
lampshade stando no kasa
land (*not sea*) tochi; **when does the plane land?** hikōki wa its chakurik shi-mass ka?
landscape keshki
lane (*on motorway*) shasen; **a country lane** inaka no komichi
language: the Japanese language Nihon-go; **the English language** Eigo; **a foreign language** gaikokugo; **polite language** teinei na kotoba; **everyday language** nichijōgo; **vulgar language** zokugo
language course gogaku-kōss
large ōkī
laryngitis kōtōen
last (*final*) saigo (no); **last year** kyonen; **last Wednesday** senshū no suiyōbi; **last night** yūbe; **when's the last bus?** saishū bass wa nan-ji dess ka?; **one last drink** saigo no ip-pai; **when were you last in London?** saikin' its Rondon ni irash-shai-mashta ka?; **at last!** tōtō!; **how long does it last?** its made tsuzuki-mass ka?
last name myōji
late osoi; **sorry I'm late** okurete sumi-masen; **don't be late** okurenaide kudasai; **the bus was late** bass ga okure-mashta; **we'll be back late** watashtachi wa osoku kaeri-mass; **it's getting late** mō osoi dess; **is it that late!** mō kon-na jikan dess ka!; **it's too late now** mō oso-sugi-mass; **I'm a late riser** watashi wa asa-nebō dess
lately saikin
later ato de; **later on** ato de; **I'll come back later** ato de kaeri-mass; **see you later** ja mata; **no later than Tuesday** kayōbi made ni
latest: the latest news saikin no nyūss; **at the latest** osoktomo
laugh (*verb*) warau; (*noun*) warai; **don't laugh** warawanaide; **it's no laughing matter** waraigoto ja ari-masen
launderette, laundromat koin-randorī
laundry (*clothes*) sentak-mono; (*place*) sentaku-ya; **could you get the laundry done?** sentak shte kure-masen ka?
lavatory otearai
law hōrits; **against the law** hōrits ni hanshte
lawn shibahu
lawyer ben-goshi
laxative gezai
lay-by dōro-giwa no chūshajō
laze around: I just want to laze around chot-to nombiri shtai to omoi-mass
lazy namake-mono; **don't be lazy** namakenaide; **a nice lazy holiday** nonki na ī kyūka
lead (*electrical*) kōdo; **where does this road lead?** kono michi wa doko e iki-mass ka?
leaf konoha
leaflet chirashi; **do you have any leaflets on ...?** ... no chirashi ga ari-mass ka?
leak moru; **the roof leaks** amamori ga shi-mass
learn: I want to learn ... ... ga narai-

tain dess
learner: I'm just a learner narai-
hajimeta bakari dess
lease (*verb*) chin-gashi suru
least: not in the least zenzen; **at least**
50 skunaktomo gojū dess
leather kawa
leave: when does the bus leave? bass
wa nan-ji ni de-mass ka?; **I leave**
tomorrow ashta de-mass; **he left this**
morning kare wa kesa de-mashta;
may I leave this here? koko ni oite
mo ī dess ka?; **I left my bag in the**
bar bā ni kaban' o wasure-mashta;
she left her bag here kanojo wa
kaban' o koko ni wasure-mashta;
leave the window open please mado
o aketoite kure-masen ka?; **there's**
not much left amari nokot-te i-
masen; **I've hardly any money left**
okane wa hotondo nokot-te i-masen;
I'll leave it up to you anata shidai
dess
lecherous skebei (na)
left hidari; **on the left** hidari ni
left-hand drive hidari-gawa unten
left-handed hidari handoru (no)
left luggage office tenimotsu
azukarisho
left wing (*noun: in politics*) sayok
leg ashi
legal hōritsjō (no)
lemon remon
lemonade remonēdo
lemon tea remon tī
lend: would you lend me your ...?
anata no ... o kashte kure-masen ka?
lens (*of camera, contact lens*) renz
lens cap renz no huta
lesbian resubian
less: less than an hour ichi-jikan' ika;
less than that sore ika; **less hot**
son-na ni atsku ari-masen
lesson jugyō; **do you give lessons?**
kojin-kyōju shi-mass ka?
let: would you let me use it? sore o
tskawasete kure-masen ka?; **will you**
let me know? shirasete kure-masen
ka?; **I'll let you know** oshirase shi-
mass; **let me try** sasete kudasai; **let**
me go! hanashte kure!; **let's leave**
now ima iki-mashō; **let's not go yet**
mada i-mashō; **will you let me off**

at ...? ... de oroshte kure-masen ka?;
rooms to let kashibeya
letter (*in mail*) tegami; (*of alphabet*)
moji; **are there any letters for me?**
watashi ni tegami ga ari-mass ka?
letterbox tegami-uke
lettuce retass
level crossing humikiri
lever (*noun*) rebā
liable (*responsible*) sekininkan no aru
liberated: a liberated woman
shimpo-teki na josei
library toshokan
licence, license menkyo
license plate (*on car*) nambā purēto
lid huta
lie (*untruth*) uso; **can he lie down for**
a while? kare wa skoshi yoko ni
nare-mass ka?; **I want to go and lie**
down it-te yoko ni nari-tai to omoi-
mass
lie-in: I'm going to have a lie-in
tomorrow ashta zut-to nete iru
tsmori dess
life seikats; **not on your life!** zet-tai
dame!; **that's life!** sore ga jinsei sa!
lifebelt kyūmei beruto
lifeboat kyūmei bōto
life insurance seimei hoken
life jacket kyūmei jaket-to
lift (*in hotel etc*) erebētā; **could you**
give me a lift? nosete kure-masen
ka?; **do you want a lift?** nosete age-
mashō ka?; **thanks for the lift**
nosete kudasat-te arigatō; **I got a lift**
nosete morai-mashta
light hikari; (*electrical*) denki; (*not*
heavy) karui; **the light was on** denki
ga tsuite i-mashta; **do you have a**
light? (*for cigarette*) mat-chi o mot-te
i-mass ka?; **a light meal** karui
shokuji; **light blue** usui ao (no)
light bulb denkyū
lighter (*for cigarette*) raitā
lighthouse tōdai
light meter roshuts-kei
lightning inabikari
like: I'd like a ... ... ga hoshī dess;
I'd like to ... sh-tai dess (*see page*
106); **would you like a ...?** ... wa
ikaga dess ka? **would you like to**
come too? anata mo iki-masen ka?;
I'd like to sō sh-tai dess; **I like it** ski

dess; **I like you** anata ga ski dess; **I don't like it** ski ja ari-masen; **he doesn't like it** ski ja ari-masen; **do you like ...?** ... ga ski dess ka?; **I like swimming** suiei ga ski dess; **OK, if you like** ja, ī dess yo; **what's it like?** dō yū kanji dess ka?; **do it like this** kono yō ni shte kudasai; **one like that** sō yū no hitots

lily yuri

limbless Buddha figure daruma

lime cordial, lime juice raim jūss

line (*on paper, telephone*) sen; (*of people*) rets; **would you give me a line?** (*telephone*) tsunaide kure-masen ka?

linen (*for beds*) shīts to makura kabā

linguist gogak ni tsyoi hito; **I'm no linguist** gogak wa nigate dess

lining uraji

lip kuchibiru

lip brush rip-p burash

lip gloss rip-p guross

lip salve rip-p kurīm

lipstick kuchibeni

liqueur rikyūru

liquor arukōru

liquor store saka-ya

list risto

listen: I'd like to listen to ... ... ga kiki-tai to omoi-mass; **listen!** kīte kudasai!

litre, liter rit-toru; *see page 120*

literature bun-gak; **ancient literature** kodai bun-gak; **modern literature** gendai bun-gak

litter (*rubbish*) gomi

little skoshi; **just a little, thanks** hon no skoshi, arigatō; **just a very little** hon no skoshi dake; **a little cream** kurīm skoshi; **a little more** mō skoshi; **a little better** (*health*) skoshi yok nari-mashta; **that's too little** (*not enough*) skuna-sugi-mass

live: I live in ... ... ni sunde i-mass; **where do you live?** doko ni sunde i-mass ka?; **where does he live?** kare wa doko ni sunde i-mass ka?; **we live together** ish-sho ni sunde i-mass

lively (*person, town*) iki-iki shta

liver (*in body, food*) kanzō

lizard tokage

loaf pan' ik-kin

lobby (*of hotel*) robī

lobster ise-ebi

local: a local speciality chihō no meibuts; **a local newspaper** chihō no shimbun; **a local restaurant** chihō no restoran

lock (*noun*) kagi; **it's locked** kagi ga kakat-te i-mass; **I locked myself out of my room** jibun no heya o rok-k shte shimai-mashta

locker (*for luggage etc*) rok-kā

log: I slept like a log gus-suri nemuri-mashta

lollipop bō-tski kyandē

London Rondon

lonely sabishī; **are you lonely?** sabishī dess ka?

long nagai; **how long does it take?** dono kurai kakari-mass ka?; **is it a long way?** tōi dess ka?; **a long time** nagai aida; **I won't be long** sugu kaeri-mass; **don't be long** hayak shte kudasai; **that was long ago** mō zuibun mae no koto dess; **I'd like to stay longer** mot-to nagaku i-tai to omoi-mass; **long time no see!** hisashiburi dess ne!; **so long!** ja ne!

long distance call chōkyori denwa

loo: where's the loo? otearai wa doko dess ka?; **I want to go to the loo** otearai ni iki-tai dess

look: that looks good (*food*) sore wa oishi-sō dess; **you look tired** tskarete iru yō dess; **I'm just looking, thanks** miteru dake dess, arigatō; **you don't look your age** anata no toshi ni wa mie-masen' yo; **look at him** kare o mite; **I'm looking for ... ...** o sagashte i-mass; **look out!** ki o tskete!; **can I have a look?** chot-to misete kure-masen ka?; **can I have a look around?** mite mawat-te mo ī dess ka?

loose (*button, handle etc*) yurui

loose change komakai okane

lorry torak-k

lorry driver torak-k no untenshu

lose nakuss; **I've lost my ...** watashi no ... o nakshi-mashta; **I'm lost** mayot-te shimai-mashta

lost property office, lost and found ishits-buts tori-atskaijo

lot: a lot, lots taksan; **not a lot** ōku ari-masen; **a lot of money** okane ga taksan; **a lot of women** josei ga taksan; **a lot cooler** zut-to suzushī dess; **I like it a lot** totemo ski dess; **is it a lot further?** mot-to tōi dess ka?; **I'll take the (whole) lot** zembu kai-mass

lotion rōshon

lotus hass

loud sawagashī; **the music is rather loud** on-gaku wa chot-to sawagashī dess

lounge (in house, hotel) raunji

lousy (meal, hotel, holiday, weather) hidoi

love: I love you anata ga ski; **he's fallen in love** kare wa koi shte i-mass; **I love Japan** Nihon ga daiski dess

lovely (meal, view, weather, present etc)

steki (na)

low (prices) yasui; (bridge) hikui

LP erupī

luck un; **hard luck!** oainik-sama!; **good luck!** gud-do rak-k!; **just my luck!** mata shkujit-ta!; **it was pure luck** hontō ni tsuite i-mashta

lucky: that's lucky! un ga yokat-ta ne!

lucky charm omamori

luggage nimots

lumbago yōtsū

lump (medical) kobu

lunar calendar kyūreki

lunch chūshok

lungs hai

luxurious (hotel, furnishings) zeitak (na)

luxury zeitak

M

macho totemo otokop-poi

mad kichigai (no)

madam ok-san; **thank you, madam** arigatō gozai-mass

magazine zash-shi

magnificent (view, day, meal) subarashī

maid otetsdai-san

maiden name kyūsei

mail yūbim-buts; **is there any mail for me?** yūbin ga kite i-mass ka?; **where can I mail this?** doko de tōkan deki-mass ka?

mailbox posto

main omo (na); **main points** omo na ten; **where's the main post office?** chūō-yūbin-kyok wa doko dess ka?; **Tokyo's main streets are always crowded** Tōkyō no omo na tōri wa itsmo konde i-mass

main road ōdōri

make tsukuru; **do you make them yourself?** jibun de tskuri-mass ka?; **it's very well made** totemo yok dekite i-mass; **what does that make altogether?** zembu de ikura dess

ka?; **I make it only 500 yen** tat-ta gohyaku en dess; **made in Japan** Nihonsei (no)

make-up keshō

make-up remover keshō otoshi

Malaysia Marēshia

Malaysian (adjective) Marēshia (no); (person) Marēshia-jin

male chauvinist pig otoko chūshin na yats

man otoko no hito

manager manējā; **may I see the manager?** manējā ni awasete kudasai

manicure manikyua

manufacture (verb) seizō suru

many taksan (no); **not many** taksan ja nak

map: a map of ... ... no chiz; **it's not on this map** kono chiz ni not-te i-masen

maple momiji

marble (noun) dairiseki

March san-gats

marijuana marifana

mark: there's a mark on it kiz ga

ari-mass; **could you mark it on the map for me?** chiz ni sono shirushi o tskete kure-masen ka?

market (*noun*) ichiba; (*in business*) shijō; **the European market** Yōroppa shijō

marmalade māmarēdo

married: are you married? kek-kon shte i-mass ka?; **I'm married** kek-kon shte i-mass

martial arts budō

mascara maskara

mass misa; **I'd like to go to mass** misa ni iki-tai dess

massage mass-sāji

mast masto

masterpiece kess-sak

mat: straw mat tatami

match (*for cigarettes*) mat-chi; (*sports*) shiai

material (*cloth*) nunoji

matter: it doesn't matter dō demo ī dess; **what's the matter?** dō shtan dess ka?

mattress mat-toress

maximum (*noun*) saidaigen

May go-gats

may: may I have another bottle? mō ip-pon' onegai-shi-mass; **may I?** yoroshī dess ka?; *see page 107*

maybe sō kamo shire-masen; **maybe not** sō ja nai kamo shire-masen

mayonnaise mayonēz

mayor shichō

me watashi; **it's for me** watashi no dess; **it's me** watashi dess; **me too** watashi mo; **come with me** ish-sho ni kite kudasai; *see page 100*

meal shokuji; **that was an excellent meal** totemo oishī shokuji deshta; **does that include meals?** shokuji-tski dess ka?

mean: what does this word mean? kono kotoba wa dō yū imi dess ka?; **what does he mean?** kare wa nani o it-te irun dess ka?

measles hashka; **German measles** hūshin

measurements sumpō

meat nik

mechanic shūrikō; **do you have a mechanic here?** shūrikō wa koko ni i-mass ka?

medicine ksuri

medieval chūsei (no)

medium (*adjective*) chūgurai (no)

medium-rare (*steak*) midiam reya

medium-sized chūgurai (no); (*clothes*) em saiz (no); (*vehicles*) chūgata

meet: pleased to meet you hajime-mashte; **where shall we meet?** doko de ai-mashō ka?; **let's meet up again** mata ai-mashō

meeting (*business etc*) kaigi

meeting place machi-awase-basho

melon meron

member membā; **I'd like to become a member** membā ni nari-tai dess

men dansei

mend: can you mend this? kore o naoshte kure-masen ka?

men's room dansei-yō otearai

mention: don't mention it dō itashi-mashte

menu menyū; **may I have the menu please?** menyū onegai-shi-mass

mess yogore

message: are there any messages for me? mess-sēji ga ari-mass ka?; **I'd like to leave a message for ... ...**-san ni mess-sēji o onegai-shi-mass

metal (*noun*) kinzok

metre, meter mētoru; *see page 119*

microwave oven denshi renji

midday: at midday mahiru ni

middle: in the middle man-naka ni; **in the middle of the road** dōro no man-naka ni

midnight: at midnight mayonaka ni

might: I might want to stay another 2 days mō hutska taizai suru kamo shire-masen; **you might have warned me!** it-te kurete mo yokat-ta no ni!

migraine henzutsū

mild (*taste*) maroyaka (na); (*weather*) atatakai

mile mairu; **that's miles away!** totemo tōi dess; *see page 119*

military (*adjective*) guntai (no)

milk miruk

milkshake miruk-sēki

millimetre, millimeter mirimētoru; *see page 119*

minced meat minchi

mind: I don't mind ī dess yo; **would**

you mind if I smoke? tabako o sutte mo ī dess ka?; **never mind** daijōbu dess; **I've changed my mind** ki ga kawari-mashta; *see page XYZ*
mine: it's mine watashi no dess; *see page 101*
mineral water mineraru uōtā
minimum (*adjective*) saitei (no)
mint (*sweet*) minto
minus mainass; **minus 2 degrees** mainass ni-do
minute hun; **in a minute** sugu; **just a minute** chot-to mat-te kudasai
mirror kagami
Miss ... ...-san; **Miss Higgins** Higinzsan; *see page 114*
miss: I miss you anata ga inakte sabishī dess; **there's a ... missing ...** ga miatari-masen; **we missed the bus** bass ni nori-okure-mashta
missionary senkyōshi
mist kiri
mistake machigai; **I think there's a mistake here** koko ni machigai ga aru to omoi-mass
misunderstanding gokai
mixture kon-gō-buts
mix-up: there's been some sort of mix-up with ... ... no koto de gokai ga aru yō dess
moat hori; (*outer*) sotobori; (*inner*) uchibori
modern modan (na); **a modern art gallery** kindai bijutskan
moisturizer (*cosmetic*) moischaraizā
moment shunkan; **I won't be a moment** chot-to mat-te kudasai
monastery sōin
Monday getsyōbi
money okane; **I don't have any money** okane ga ari-masen; **do you take English/American money?** Igiriss/Amerika no okane o tori-mass ka?
month: one month ik-kagets; **two months** ni-kagets; **three months** san-kagets; **for two months** ni-kagets-kan; **in two months' time** ni-kagets go ni; **two months ago** ni-kagets mae ni; **this month** kon-gets; **next month** raigets; **last month** sengets; **every month** maitski
monument kinen-hi

moon tski
moon viewing tskimi
moped tansha
more mot-to; **may I have some more?** mot-to itadake-mass ka?; **more water, please** mot-to omizu onegai-shi-mass; **no more** mō kek-kō dess; **more expensive** mot-to takai dess; **more than 50** gojū ijō; **more than that** sore ijō; **a lot more** mot-to taksan; **not any more** mō ...-masen; **I don't stay there any more** mō soko ni wa tomat-te i-masen
morning asa; **good morning** ohayō gozai-mass; **this morning** kasa; **in the morning** gozen-chū; (*early*) asa ni
morning glory asagao
mosquito ka
mosquito net kaya
most: I like this one most kore ga ichi-ban ski dess; **most of the time** taitei; **most of the hotels** taitei no hoteru
mother okā-san; **my mother** haha
motif (*in pattern*) mochīf
motor mōtā
motorbike ōtobai
motorboat mōtābōto
motorist unten suru hito
motorway kōsok-dōro
motor yacht enjin-tski yot-to
Mount Fuji Huji-san
mountain yama; **up in the mountains** yama no ue ni; **a mountain village** sanson
mouse nezumi
moustache kuchi-hige
mouth kuchi
move: he's moved to another hotel kare wa hoka no hoteru ni utsuri-mashta; **could you move your car?** kuruma o ugokashte kure-masen ka?
movie eiga; **let's go to the movies** eiga ni iki-mashō
movie camera satsueiki
movie theater eigakan
moving: a very moving tune totemo kandō-teki na kyok
Mr ... ...-san; **Mr Forsyth** Fōsaiss-san; *see page 114*
Mrs ... ...-san; **Mrs Burdett** Bādet-to-

san; *see page 114*
Ms ... ...-san; **Ms Kirby** Kābī-san; *see page 114*
much taksan (no); **much better** zut-to ī dess; **much cooler** zut-to suzushī dess; **not much** skoshi; **not so much** sore hodo demo ari-masen
muffler (*on car*) shō-onki
mug: I've been mugged gōtō ni osoware-mashta
mumps otahuku-kaze
murals hekiga
muscle kin-nik
museum hakubutskan
mushroom (*white button*) mash-shurūm; (*Chinese*) shītake
music on-gak; **guitar music** gitā no on-gak; **do you have the sheet music for ...?** ... no gak-hu ga ari-mass ka?
musician on-gaku-ka
mussels mūru-gai
must: I must ... ...-nakte wa ike-masen; **I must go** (*have to*) ika-nakte wa nari-masen; (*would like*) zehi iki-tai dess; **I mustn't drink ...** ... o node wa ike-masen; **you mustn't forget** wasurete wa ike-masen
mustache kuchi-hige
mustard karashi
my watashi no; *see page 113*
myself: I'll do it myself jibun de shi-mass
myth shinwa

N

nail (*of finger*) tsme; (*in wood*) kugi
nail clippers tsme-kiri
nailfile tsme-yō yasuri
nail polish manikyua
nail polish remover jokō-eki
nail scissors tsme-kiri-yō hasami
naked hadaka (no)
name namae; **what's your name?** onamae wa nan to osh-shai-mass ka?; **what's its name?** namae wa nan dess ka?; **my name is ...** watashi no namae wa ... dess
name card meishi
nap hirune; **he's having a nap** kare wa hirune-chū dess
napkin (*serviette*) napkin
nappy omuts
narrow (*road*) semai
nasty (*taste, person, weather*) iya (na); (*cut*) hidoi
national kuni (no)
national lottery takarakuji
nationality kokseki
natural shizen (na)
naturally (*of course*) mochiron
nature (*trees etc*) shizen
nausea hakike
near ... ... no soba; **near the window** mado no soba; **is it near here?** sore wa koko no chikak dess ka?; **do you go near ...?** ... no chikaku e iki-mass ka?; **where is the nearest ...?** ichi-ban chikai ... wa doko dess ka?
nearby chikai
nearly hotondo; **nearly 10,000 yen** ichi-man'en chikak; **I've nearly finished** hotondo sumi-mashta
neat (*room etc*) kichinto shta; (*drink*) storēto (no)
necessary hitsyō (na); **is it necessary to ...?** ... hitsyō ga ari-mass ka?; **it's not necessary** sono hitsyō wa ari-masen
neck (*of body, of dress, shirt*) kubi
necklace nek-kuress
necktie nektai
need iru; **I need a ...** ... ga iri-mass; **do I need a ...?** ... ga iri-mass ka?; **it needs more salt/pepper** mot-to shio/koshō ga iri-mass; **there's no need** sono hitsyō wa ari-masen; **there's no need to shout!** sakebu koto wa ari-masen

needle hari
negative (*film*) nega
neighbo(u)r kinjo no hito
neighbo(u)rhood kinjo
neither: neither of us watashtachi no dare demo nai; **neither one (of them)** (*people*) dare demo nai; (*objects*) dore demo nai; **neither ... nor ... ...** demo ... demo nai; **neither do I** watashi mo sō dess; **neither does he** kare mo sō dess
nephew oigo-san; **my nephew** oi
nervous shinkei-shits (na)
net (*fishing*) ami; (*sports*) net-to
neurotic shinkei-shō (no)
neutral (*gear*) nyūtoraru
never kesh-shte ...-masen; **he never smiles** kare wa kesh-shte warai-masen; **never!** masaka; *see page 110*
new atarashī
news nyūss; **is there any news?** nani ka atarashī koto ga ari-mass ka?
newspaper shimbun; **do you have any English newspapers?** eiji shimbun ga ari-mass ka?
newsstand shimbun hambaisho
New Year oshōgats; **Happy New Year** ake-mashte omedetō gozai-mass; **New Year's Eve** ōmisoka; **New Year's Day** gantan; **New Year postcard** nen-ga-jō; **New Year visit to a shrine** hatsmōde; **New Year pine decorations** kadomats
New York Nyū Yōk
New Zealand Nyū Jīrando
New Zealander Nyū Jīrando-jin
next tsugi (no); **it's at the next corner** tsugi no kado ni ari-mass; **next week** raishū; **next Monday** raishū no getsyōbi; **next to the post office** yūbinkyok no tonari; **the one next to that** sono tonari no
nextdoor (*adverb*) tonari (ni); (*adjective*) tonari (no)
next of kin kinshin-sha
nice (*person, town, day*) ī; (*meal*) oishī; **that's very nice of you** goshinsets-sama; **a nice cold drink** tsmetakte oishī nomimono
nickname nik-kunēm
niece meigo-san; **my niece** mei
night yoru; **for one night** (*in hotel*) ip-pak; **for three nights** (*in hotel*)

sam-pak; **good night** oyasumi-nasai; **at night** yoru ni
nightcap (*drink*) nezake
nightclub naitokurab
nightdress nemaki
night flight yoru no bin
nightie nemaki
night-life yoru no gorak
nightmare akumu
night porter yoru no momban
no (*answer*) īe; **I've no money/time** okane/jikan ga ari-masen; **there's no more** mō nokot-te i-masen; **no more than ... ...** ika; **oh no!** (*upset*) masaka; *see page 114*
nobody dare mo ...-masen; **nobody was there** dare mo i-masen deshta; **I saw nobody** dare ni mo ai-masen deshta; *see page 110*
noise sō-on
noisy urusai; **it's too noisy** urusa-sugi-mass
non-alcoholic (*drink*) arukōru nashi (no)
none (*people*) dare mo ...-masen; (*objects*) dore mo ...-masen; **I like none of them** dare/dore mo ski ja ari-masen; *see page 110*
nonsense baka-geta
non-smoking (*compartment, section of plane*) kin'en (no)
non-stop (*travel*) chok-kō (no)
no-one dare mo ...-masen; **no-one is at home** dare mo ie ni i-masen; *see page 110*
nor: nor do I watashi mo sō dess; **nor does he** kare mo sō dess; *see page 110*
normal seijō (na)
north kita; **to the north** kita no hō e
northeast hoktō; **to the northeast** hoktō e
Northern Ireland Kita Airurando
northwest hoksei; **to the northwest** hoksei e
Norway Noruē
nose hana; **my nose is bleeding** hana-ji ga dete i-mass
not -masen; **I don't smoke** watashi wa tabako o sui-masen; **he didn't say anything** kare wa nani mo ī-masen deshta; **it's not important** sore wa jūyō na koto ja ari-masen; **not that**

one sore ja ari-masen; **not for me** watashi wa kek-kō dess; *see page 110*
note (*bank note*) shihei; (*written message etc*) den-gon
notebook techō; (*exercise book*) nōto
nothing nani mo ...-masen; **I bought nothing** nani mo kai-masen deshta; **nothing is missing** nani mo nakunat-te i-masen
November jūichi-gats
now ima; **not now** ima ja ari-masen
nowhere doko ni mo ...-masen; **we went nowhere yesterday** kinō wa doko ni mo iki-masen deshta

nuisance: he's being a nuisance (*pestering woman etc*) kare wa yak-kai na hito dess
numb (*limb etc*) shibireta
number (*figure*) kaz; **what number?** ban-gō wa?
number plates nambā purēto
nurse kan-gohu
nursery (*at airport etc, for children*) yūgi-shits; (*for babies and toddlers*) junyū-shits
nut nat-ts; (*for bolt*) nat-to
nutter: he's a nutter (*is crazy*) kare wa kawari-mono dess

O

obligatory kyōsei-teki (na)
oblige: much obliged (*thank you*) osore-iri-mass
obnoxious (*person*) hata-meiwak (na)
obvious akiraka (na); **that's obvious** sore wa akiraka dess
occasionally tokidoki
Occident Seiyō
Occidental (*adjective*) Seiyō (no)
o'clock *see page 117*
October jū-gats
octopus tako
odd (*strange*) kawat-ta; (*number*) kisū
of: of ... ... no; **the name of the hotel** hoteru no namae; **have one of mine** watashi no o dōzo; *see page 104*
off: 20% off ni-waribiki; **the lights were off** denki wa kiete i-mashta; **just off the main road** ōdōri kara chot-to hazurete
offend: don't be offended ki o waruk shinaide kudasai
offerings sonaemono
office (*place of work*) jimusho
officer (*said to policeman*) omawari-san
official (*noun*) shoku-in; **is that official?** sore wa kōshki dess ka?
off-licence saka-ya
off-season kisets-hazure (no)
often yok; **not often** met-ta ni

oil (*for car*) oiru; (*for cooking*) abura; (*for salad*) sarada oiru; **it's losing oil** oiru ga morete i-mass; **will you change the oil?** oiru o kōkan shte kure-masen ka?; **the oil light's flashing** oiru ramp ga tem-mets shte i-mass
oil painting abura-e
oil pressure yu-ats
ointment nankō
OK ōkē; **are you OK?** daijōbu dess ka?; **that's OK thanks** sore de kek-kō dess arigatō; **is that OK?** (*is that good?*) sore de ī dess ka?; (*can I?*) sō shte ī dess ka?; **that's OK by me** watashi wa sore de ī dess; **OK, I understand** hai wakari-mashta
old (*person*) toshiyori (no); (*thing*) hurui; **how old are you?** nan-sai dess ka?; **I'm 25 years old** nijūgo-sai dess
old-age pensioner yōrō nenkin seikats-sha
old-fashioned kyūshki (na)
old town (*old part of town*) kyū-shigai
omlet(te) omurets
on: on ... ... no ue; **on the roof** yane no ue; **on the beach** hamabe de; **on Friday** kin'yōbi ni; **on television** terebi de; **I don't have it on me** ima

mot-te i-masen; **this drink's on me**
kono nomimono wa watashi-mochi
dess; **a book on Kyoto** Kyōto ni
kansuru hon; **the warning light
comes on** kiken shin-gō ga tski-
mass; **the light was on** denki wa
tsuite i-mashta; **what's on in town?**
machi de wa nani o yat-te i-mass
ka?; **it's just not on!** (*not acceptable*)
sore wa dame dess!

once (*one time*) ik-kai; (*formerly*) mae
ni ichido; **at once** (*immediately*) sugu

one hitots; **that one** sore; **the green
one** midori no; **the one with the
black skirt on** kuroi skāto no hito;
the one in the blue shirt aoi shats
no hito

onion tamanegi

only: only ... ... dake; **only one** hitots
dake; **only once** ik-kai dake; **it's
only 9 o'clock** mada ku-ji dess; **I've
only just arrived** mada tsuita bakari
dess

open (*adjective*) hiraita; **when do you
open?** itsu ake-mass ka?; **in the open**
(*in open air*) kogai de; **it won't open**
aki-masen

opening times hirak jikok

opera opera

operation (*medical*) shujuts

operator (*telephone*) kōkanshu

opportunity kikai

opposite: opposite the church/theatre
kyōkai/gekijō no mukai-gawa; **it's
directly opposite** chōdo mamukai
dess

oppressive (*heat*) udaru-yō (na)

optician megane-ya

optimistic rak-kan-teki (na)

optional zui-i (no)

or mata wa

oracle: written oracle omikuji

orange (*fruit*) orenji; (*colour*) orenji-iro
(no)

orange juice orenji jūss

orchestra ōkestora

order chūmon suru; **could we order
now?** (*in restaurant*) chūmon shte mo
ī dess ka?; **I've already ordered** mō
chūmon shte ari-mass; **I didn't
order that** sore o chūmon shi-masen
deshta; **it's out of order** (*lift etc*)
kowarete i-mass; **thank you for your**

order gochūmon itadaite arigatō
gozai-mass

ordinary hutsū (no)

organization (*company*) soshki

organize keikak suru; **could you
organize it?** sore o keikak shte
kure-masen ka?

Orient Tōyō

Oriental (*adjective*) Tōyō (no); (*person*)
Tōyō-jin

original (*adjective*) doksō-teki (na); **is
it an original?** sore wa gembuts dess
ka?

ornament kazarimono

ostentatious (*clothes, colour etc*) hade
(na)

other hoka no; **the other waiter** hoka
no uētā; **the other one** hoka no; **do
you have any others?** hoka no mo
ari-mass ka?; **some other time,
thanks** mata bets no toki ni shte
kudasai

otherwise moshi sō de nakereba

ouch! aita!

ought: he ought to be here soon kare
wa kit-to sugu ni ki-mass

ounce *see page 120*

our watashtachi no; **our hotel**
watashtachi no hoteru; **our suitcases**
watashtachi no sūts-kēss; *see page 113*

ours watashtachi no; **that's ours** sore
wa watashtachi no dess; *see page 101*

out: he's out kare wa gaishuts-chū
dess; **get out!** dete iki-nasai; **I'm out
of money** okane ga nakunat-te
shimai-mashta; **a few kilometres out
of town** machi o sū-kiro hanarete

outdoors kogai de

outlet (*electrical*) konsento

outside soto; **can we sit outside?** soto
ni suwari-masen ka?

outskirts: on the outskirts of ... ... no
hazure ni

oven ōbun

over: over here koko ni; **over there**
asoko ni; **over 100** hyaku ijō; **I'm
burnt all over** karada-jū yake-
mashta; **the holiday's over** kyūka wa
owari-mashta

overcharge: you've overcharged me
kajō ni seikyū shte i-mass

overcoat ōbā

overcooked (*boiled*) ni-sugita; (*fried*)

yaki-sugita
overexposed (*photograph*) roshuts-kajō (no)
overheat: it's overheating (*car*) ōbāhīto shte i-mass
overland (*travel*) rikuro de
overlook: overlooking the sea umi o miharass
overnight (*travel*) ip-pak (no)
overseas kaigai (no); **overseas market** kaigai shijō; **overseas travel** kaigai ryokō; **overseas telephone call** koksai denwa

oversleep: I overslept ne-sugoshi-mashta
overtake (*pass*) oinuk
overweight (*person*) hutori-sugi; (*luggage*) jūryō-chōka
owe: how much do I owe you? (*in shop*) ikura dess ka?
own: my own ... watashi jishin no ...; **are you on your own?** ohitori dess ka?; **I'm on my own** hitori dess
owner mochinushi
oyster kaki

P

Pacific Ocean Taiheiyō
pack: a pack of cigarettes tabako hito-hako; **I'll go and pack** nizukuri o shte ki-mass
package (*at post office*) kozutsmi
package holiday pak-kēji horidē
package tour pak-kēji tsuā
packed lunch bentō
packed out: the place was packed out konde i-mashta
packet hako; **a packet of cigarettes** tabako hito-hako
paddy field suiden
padlock (*noun*) nankin-jō
page (*of book*) pēji; **could you page Mr ...?** ...-san' o yobidashte kuremasen ka?
pagoda tō; **five-storey pagoda** gojū no tō
pain itami; **I have a pain here** koko ga itai dess
painful itai
painkillers itamidome
paint (*noun*) (*art*) enogu; (*on building*) penki; (*on car*) peinto; **I'm going to do some painting** (*artist*) e o kak tsmori dess
paintbrush (*artist's*) ehude
painting e
pair: a pair of ... hito-kumi no ...
pajamas pajama

Pakistan Pakistan
Pakistani (*adjective*) Pakistan (no); (*person*) Pakistan-jin
pal nakama
palace kyūden
pale (*face*) aojiroi; (*colour*) usu-; **pale blue** usu-aoi; **you look pale** anata wa kao-iro ga warui dess
palpitations dōki
pancake hot-to-kēki
panic: don't panic awatenaide
panties pantī
pants (*trousers*) zubon; (*underpants*) pants
panty girdle gādoru
pantyhose pantī stok-king-g
paper kami; (*newspaper*) shimbun; **a piece of paper** kami ichi-mai
paper folding origami
paper handkerchiefs tish-shū pēpā
paraffin tōyu
parallel: parallel to ... ... to heikō ni
parasol higasa
parcel kozutsmi
pardon (me)? (*didn't understand*) nan to ī-mashta ka?
parents goryōshin; **my parents** ryōshin
parents-in-law giri no goryōshin; **my parents-in-law** giri no ryōshin
park (*noun*) kōen; **where can I park?**

doko ni chūsha deki-mass ka?;
there's nowhere to park chūsha
suru tokoro wa ari-masen
parka anorak-k
parking lights bitō
parking lot chūshajō
**parking place: there's a parking
place!** asoko ni chūsha deki-mass!
part (*noun*) bubun
partner (*boyfriend, girlfriend etc*) tsure;
(*in business*) kyōdō kei-ei-sha
party (*group*) dantai; (*celebration*) pātī;
let's have a party pātī o shi-mashō
pass (*in mountains*) tōge; (*verb: overtake*) oinuk; **he passed out** kare wa
kizets shi-mashta; **he made a pass at
me** kare wa watashi ni narenareshku
shi-mashta
passable (*road*) tōreru
passenger jōkyak
passport paspōto
past: in the past mae ni; **just past the
bank/lights** ginkō/shin-gō no sugu
mukō; *see page 117*
pastry (*dough*) pai-gawa; (*small cake*)
pēstorī
**patch: could you put a patch on
this?** kore ni tsugi o atete kure-
masen ka?
pâté pate
path komichi
patient: be patient shimbō shte
kudasai
patio naka-niwa
pattern moyō; **a dress pattern** yōsai
no katagami
paunch onaka
pavement (*sidewalk*) hodō
pay (*verb*) shiharau; **can I pay,
please?** kanjō ni shte kudasai; **it's
already paid for** mō harat-te ari-
mass; **I'll pay for this** kore wa
watashi ga harai-mass
pay phone aka-denwa
**peace and quiet: I'd like some peace
and quiet** nombiri shtai dess
peach momo
peanuts pīnat-ts
pear nashi
pearl shinju
peas gurīmpīss
peculiar (*taste, custom*) kawat-ta
pedal (*noun*) pedaru

pedestrian hokōsha
pedestrian crossing ōdan-hodō
pedestrian precinct hokōsha ten-gok
pee: I need to go for a pee toire ni
iki-tai dess; (*said by girls, children*)
oshik-ko ni iki-tai dess
peeping Tom chikan
pen pen; **do you have a pen?** pen ga
ari-mass ka?
pencil empits
penfriend pemparu; **shall we be pen-
friends?** pemparu ni nari-mashō ka?
penicillin penishirin
penknife kogatana
pen pal pemparu
pensioner nenkin juryō-sha
people hito; **a lot of people** ōzei no
hito; **the Japanese people** Nihon no
hito
pepper (*spice*) koshō; **green pepper**
pīman; **red pepper** pimento
peppermint (*sweet*) pepāminto
per: per night hito-ban ni tski; **how
much per hour?** ichi-jikan ni tski
ikura deshō ka?
per cent pāsento
perfect kampeki (na)
perfume kōsui
perhaps tabun
period (*of time*) jiki; (*era*) jidai; **Edo
era** Edo jidai; (*menstruation*) seiri
perm pāma
permit (*noun*) kyoka
persimmon kaki
person hito
pessimistic hikan-teki (na)
petrol gasorin
petrol can sekiyu kan
petrol station gasorin stando
petrol tank (*in car*) nenryō tank
pharmacy yak-kyok
Philippino (*adjective*) Firipin (no);
(*person*) Firipin-jin
Philippines Firipin
phone *see* **telephone**
phonecard fōn-kādo
photogenic shashin'utsuri ga ī
photograph (*noun*) shashin; **would
you take a photograph of us?**
shashin tot-te kure-masen ka?
photographer shashin-ka
phrase hyōgen; **a useful phrase** benri
na hyōgen

phrasebook hyōgen-shū
pianist pianisto
piano piano
pickpocket suri
pick up: when can I pick them up?
(*clothes from laundry etc*) its deki-
agari-mass ka?; **will you come and
pick me up?** mukae ni kite kure-
masen ka?
picnic (*noun*) pikunik-k
picture e; (*photo*) shashin
pie (*meat*) mīto pai; (*fruit*) pai
piece: a piece of ... ... hito-kire
pig buta
pigeon hato
piles (*medical*) ji
pile-up (*crash*) gekitots jiko
pill piru; **I'm on the pill** piru o
nonde i-mass
pillarbox posto
pillow makura
pillow case makura kabā
pin (*noun*) pin
pinball pachinko
pine mats
pineapple painap-puru
pineapple juice painap-puru jūss
pink pink
pint *see page 121*
pipe (*for smoking*) paip; (*for water*)
suidō-kan
pipe cleaner paip kurīnā
pipe tobacco paip tabako
pity: it's a pity zan-nen dess
pizza piza
place (*noun*) tokoro; **is this place
empty?** koko wa aite i-mass ka?;
would you keep my place for me?
koko o tot-te oite kure-masen ka?; **at
my place** watashi no tokoro de
place mat ranchom mat-to
plain (*food*) kantan (na); (*not patterned*)
muji (no)
plane hikōki
plant shokubuts
plaster cast gips
plastic puraschik-k
plastic bag binīru bukuro
plate sara
platform purat-to hōm; **which platform please?** dono purat-to hōm
dess ka?
play (*verb*) (*sports*) suru; (*music*) hik;

(*children*) asobu; (*noun: in theatre*)
shibai
playboy purēbōi
playground undōjō
pleasant kimochi no ī
please: please (do) dōzo; **yes please**
hai onegai-shi-mass; **could you
please ...?** ...-te kure-masen ka?;
could you please help me? tetsdat-te
kure-masen ka?; **please take it** dōzo
uketot-te kudasai; *see page 107*
pleasure: with pleasure yorokonde
plenty: plenty of ... taksan no ...;
that's plenty, thanks mō kek-kō dess
pleurisy rokumaku-en
pliers puraiyā
plonk (*wine*) sake; (*cheap wine*)
yasuzake
plug: (*electrical, for car*) purag; (*in
sink*) haisui-sen
plughole haisui-guchi
plum puram
plumber haikan-kō
plus (*arithmetic*) tass
p.m. gogo; **at 2.00 p.m.** gogo ni-ji ni;
at 10.00 p.m. gogo jū-ji ni; *see page
117*
pneumonia hai-en
poached egg otosh tamago
pocket poket-to; **in my pocket**
watashi no poket-to ni
pocketbook (*woman's handbag*) hando-
bag-g
pocketknife kogatana
point: could you point to it? yubi de
shimeshte kure-masen ka?; **four
point six** yon ten rok; **there's no
point** muda dess
points (*in car*) pointo
poisonous yūdok (no)
police keisats; **call the police!** keisats
o yonde kudasai
policeman keikan
police station keisats-sho
polish (*noun*) tsuya-dashi; **will you
polish my shoes?** kutsu o migaite
kure-masen ka?
polite teinei (na)
politician seiji-ka
politics seiji
polluted kitanai
pollution osen
pond ike

pony ko-uma
pool (*for swimming*) pūru; (*game*) tamatski
pool table tamatski-dai
poor (*not rich*) bimbō; (*quality*) somats (na); **poor old Taro!** kawaisō na Tarō-san
Pope Rōma hō-ō
pop music ryūkō-ka
popsicle (*tm*) aiss-kyandē
pop singer ryūkō-kashu
popular popyurā (na)
population jinkō
pork butanik
port (*for boats*) minato; (*drink*) pōto
porter (*in hotel*) pōtā; (*at station etc*) akabō
portrait pōtorēto
poser (*phoney person*) hat-tari-ya
posh (*restaurant*) gōka (na); (*people*) yūga (na)
possibility kanōsei
possible kanō (na); **is it possible to ...?** ... koto ga deki-mass ka?; **as ... as possible** dekiru dake ...
post (*noun: mail*) yūbin; **could you post this for me?** kore o tōkan shte kure-masen ka?
postbox posto
postcard hagaki
poster postā
poste restante kyok-dome
post office yūbin-kyok
pot (*cooking*) nabe
potato jaga-imo
potato chips poteto chip-p
potato salad poteto sarada
pottery (*objects*) tōki; (*workshop*) kamamoto
pound (*money*) pondo; (*weight*) paundo; *see page 120*
pour: it's pouring down dosha-buri dess
powder (*for face*) oshiroi
powdered milk kona miruk
power cut teiden
power point konsento
power station hatsdensho
practise, practice renshū; **I need to practise** renshū ga iri-mass
pram uba-guruma
prawn coctail kuruma-ebi no kakteru
prawns kuruma-ebi

prefecture ken
prefer: I prefer beer bīru no hō ga ski dess
preferably dekireba; **preferably not tomorrow** dekireba ashta de nai hō ga ī dess
pregnant ninshin shte iru
prescription (*for chemist*) shohō-sen
present (*gift*) purezento; **here's a present for you** kore o anata ni purezento shi-mass; **at present** ima wa
president (*of company*) shachō; (*of country*) daitōryō; (*of university*) gakchō
press: could you press these? kore ni airon' o kakete kure-masen ka?
pretty (*adjective*) kirei (na); **it's pretty expensive** kanari takai dess
price nedan
prickly heat asemo
priest (*Christian*) bokshi; (*Buddhist*) sōryo; (*Shinto*) kan-nushi
Prime Minister sōri-daijin
print (*noun: picture*) han-ga
printed matter insats buts
priority (*in driving*) yūsen; **who has priority?** dare ni yūsen-ken ga ari-mass ka?
prison keimusho
private: a private matter kojin-teki na koto; **a private school** shirits gak-kō; **private bath** sen'yō no huroba
prize shōhin; (*money*) shōkin
probably osorak
problem mondai; **I have a problem** komat-te i-mass; **no problem!** daijōbu!
program(me) (*TV, radio*) ban-gumi; (*schedule*) nit-tei; (*theatre, computer*) puroguram
promise: I promise yaksok shi-mass; **is that a promise?** kit-to dess ka?
pronounce hatsuon; **how do you pronounce this?** dō hatsuon shi-mass ka?
properly chanto; **it's not repaired properly** chanto shūzen shte ari-masen
prostitute baishunhu
protect mamoru
Protestant purotestanto
proud hokori ni suru; **we are very**

proud of this product kono seihin' o hokori ni shte i-mass
proverb kotowaza
prunes hosh-sumomo
public (*adjective*) kōkyō (no)
public bath sentō
public convenience kōshū benjo
public holiday saijits
pudding dezāto
pull hik; **he pulled out without indicating** hōkō shiji shinaide shasen kara de-mashta
pullover sētā
pump (*noun*) pomp
punctual jikan ga seikak (na)
puncture (*noun*) pank
puppet nin-gyō
puppet show nin-gyō shibai
puppet theatre, theater bunrak

pure (*silk etc*) junsui (na)
purple murasaki (no)
purse (*for money*) saihu; (*handbag*) hando-bag-g
push oss; **don't push in!** warikomanaide!
push-chair kuruma-iss
put ok; **where did you put ...?** ... o doko ni oki-mashta ka?; **where can I put ...?** ... o doko ni oki-mashō ka?; **could you put the lights on?** denki o tskete kure-masen ka?; **will you put the light out?** denki o keshte kure-masen ka?; **you've put the price up** neage shi-mashta ne; **could you put us up for the night?** komban watashtachi o tomete kure-masen ka?
pyjamas pajama

Q

quake jishin
quality hinshits; **poor quality** hinshits ga warui; **good quality** hinshits ga ī
quarantine bōeki-kensa; **is quarantine necessary?** bōeki-kensa no hitsyō ga ari-mass ka?
quart *see page 121*
quarter yom-bun no ichi; **quarter of an hour** jūgo-hun; **three quarters of an hour** yonjūgo-hun; *see page 117*
quay hatoba
quayside: on the quayside hatoba de
question shitsmon; **that's out of the question** sore wa mat-tak hukanō dess

queue (*noun*) gyōrets; **there was a big queue** nagai gyōrets ga dekite i-mashta
quick hayai; **that was quick** hayakatta dess; **which is the quickest way?** dore ga ichi-ban hayai hōhō dess ka?
quickly hayak
quiet (*place, hotel*) shizka (na); **be quiet!** shizka ni shte kudasai!
quinine kinīne
quite: quite a lot kanari taksan; **it's quite different** kanari chigai-mass; **I'm not quite sure** amari yok wakari-masen

R

rabbit usagi
rabies kyōkem-byō
race (*for horses*) keiba; (*for cars, runners*) rēss; **I'll race you there** asoko made kyōsō shi-mashō
racket (*sport*) raket-to
radiator (*of car*) rajiētā; (*in room*) dambō-ki
radio rajio; (*private: of taxi company etc*) musen; **on the radio** rajio de
rag (*for cleaning*) zōkin
rail: by rail denha de
rail pass teiki-ken
railroad, railway tetsdō
railroad crossing humikiri
rain (*noun*) ame; **in the rain** ame no naka de; **it's raining** ame ga hut-te i-mass
rain boots naga-guts
raincoat rēnkōto
rainy season tsuyu
rape (*noun*) hujo-bōkō
rare (*object etc*) mezurashī; (*steak*) reya
rash (*on skin*) hukidemono
rat dobu-nezumi
rate (*for changing money*) rēto; **what's the rate for the pound?** pondo to no kawase rēto wa ikura dess ka?; **what are your rates?** (*at car hire etc*) ryōkin wa ikura dess ka?
rather: it's rather late mō osoi dess; **I'd rather ...** ... no hō ga ī dess; **I'd rather have boiled rice** gohan no hō ga ī dess
raw (*meat*) nama (no)
razor (*dry, electric*) higesori
razor blades kamisori no ha
reach: within easy reach chikak ni
read yomu; **I can't read it** yome-masen; **could you read it out?** koe o dashte yonde kure-masen ka?; **I can't read Japanese** Nihon-go wa yome-masen
ready yōi ga dekita; **when will it be**

ready? its deki-mass ka?; **I'll go and get ready** yōi o shte ki-mass; **I'm not ready yet** mada yōi ga dekite i-masen
real hontō (no)
really hontō ni; **I really must go** mō hontō ni shitsurei shi-mass; **is it really necessary?** hontō ni sono hitsyō ga ari-mass ka?
realtor hudōsan'ya
rear: at the rear ushiro ni; **rear wheels** kōrin
rearview mirror bak-k mirā
reasonable (*prices*) takaku-nai; (*person*) mono-wakari ga ī; **be reasonable!** mucha o iwanaide!
receipt ryōshūsho
recently saikin
reception (*in hotel*) uketske; (*for guests*) resepshon
reception desk uketske
receptionist uketske no hito
recipe tskuri-kata; **can you give me the recipe for this?** kono tskuri-kata o oshiete kure-masen ka?
recognize ki ga tsku; **I didn't recognize it** ki ga tski-masen deshta
recommend: could you recommend ...? ... o suisen shte kure-masen ka?
record (*music*) rekōdo
record player rekōdo purēyā
red akai
red wine aka-wain
reduction (*in price*) nesage
refreshing sawayaka (na)
refrigerator reizōko
refund harai-modoshi; **do I get a refund?** harai-modoshte morae-mass ka?
region chihō
registered: by registered mail kakitome yūbin de
registration number tōrok ban-gō
relative: my relatives watashi no

shinrui

relaxing yasumaru; **its very relaxing** totemo ki ga yasumari-mass

reliable (*person, car*) shinrai dekiru

religion shūkyō

remains (*of old city etc*) kyūseki

remember: I don't remember omoidase-masen; **I remember** oboete i-mass; **do you remember?** oboete i-mass ka?

remote (*village etc*) hanareta

rent (*noun*) kari-chin; (*for apartment*) ya-chin; (*verb: car etc*) kariru; **I'd like to rent a bike/car** jitensha/kuruma o kari-tai dess

rental car renta-kā

repair (*verb*) shūzen suru; **can you repair it?** shūzen deki-mass ka?

repeat kuri-kaess; **could you repeat that?** mō ichi-do onegai-shi-mass

representative (*noun: of company*) daihyō-sha

request (*noun*) onegai

rescue (*verb*) kyūjo suru

reservation yoyak; **I have a reservation** yoyak shte ari-mass

reserve yoyak suru; **I reserved a room in the name of ...** ... no namae de heya o yoyak shi-mashta; **can I reserve a table for tonight?** komban tēburu hitots yoyak deki-mass ka?

rest (*repose*) kyūsok; (*remainder*) nokori; **I need a rest** yasumi ga iri-mass; **the rest of the group** nokori no hitotachi

restaurant restoran

restoration: Meiji Restoration Meiji Ishin

rest room (*toilet*) otearai

retired: I'm retired watashi wa intai shi-mashta

return: a return to Nagoya Nagoya made no ōhuku kip-pu o ichi-mai; **I'll return it tomorrow** ashta okaeshi shi-mass

reverse charge call uketori-nim barai no denwa

reverse gear bak-k gia

revolting huyukai (na)

rheumatism ryūmachi

rib abarabone; **a cracked rib** hibi no hait-ta abarabone

ribbon (*for hair*) ribon; (*for typewriter etc*) ink-ribon

rice (*uncooked*) kome; (*boiled*) gohan; (*fried*) yakimeshi

rice bowl chawan

rice field tambo

rich (*person*) kanemochi (no); (*food*) omoi; **it's too rich** omo-sugi-mass

ride: can you give me a ride into town? machi made nosete morat-te ī dess ka?; **thanks for the ride** nosete kurete arigatō

ridiculous: that's ridiculous bakagete i-mass

right (*correct*) tadashī; (*not left*) migi; **you're right** sono tōri dess; **you were right** anata no yū tōri deshta; **that's right** sō dess; **that can't be right** son-na haz wa ari-masen; **right!** (*I see*) naruhodo; **is this the right road for ...?** kono michi wa ... e iki-mass ka?; **on the right** migite ni; **turn right** migi e magat-te kudasai; **not right now** ima sugu ni ja ari-masen

right-hand drive migi handoru (no)

right wing (*noun: in politics*) uyok

ring (*on finger*) yubiwa; **I'll ring you** ato de denwa shi-mass

ring road kanjō dōro

ripe (*fruit*) juku-shta

rip-off: it's a rip-off son-na berabō na!; **rip-off prices** berabō na nedan

risky kiken (na); **it's too risky** sore wa kiken-sugi-mass

river kawa; **by the river** kawagishi (no)

road michi; **is this the road to ...?** kono michi wa ... e iki-mass ka?; **further down the road** kono michi o zut-to ik to

road accident kōtsū jiko

road map dōro-chiz

roadside: by the roadside dōrozoi ni

roadsign dōro hyōshki

roadwork(s) dōro kōji

roast beef rōsto bīf

rob: I've been robbed gōtō ni osoware-mashta

robe (*housecoat*) heya-gi

robot robot-to

rock (*stone*) iwa; **on the rocks** (*with ice*) onza-rok-k

rocky (*coast etc*) iwa-darake (no)
roll (*bread*) rōru
Roman Catholic rōma katorik-k
romance romanss
Rome: when in Rome ... gō ni iraba, gō ni shtagae
roof yane; **on the roof** yane no ue ni
room heya; **do you have a room?** aki-beya ga ari-mass ka?; **a room for two people** hutari-beya; **a room for three nights** hito-heya, sampak; **a room with a bathroom** huro-tski no heya; **in my room** watashi no heya de; **there's no room** yoyū ga ari-masen
room service rūm sābiss
rope rōp
rose bara
rosé (*wine*) roze
rotary rōtarī
rough (*sea, crossing*) arai; **the engine sounds a bit rough** enjin no oto ga skoshi mimi-zawari dess
roughly (*approximately*) oyoso
roulette rūret-to
round (*adjective*) marui; **it's my round** watashi no ban dess
roundabout (*for traffic*) rōtarī
round-trip: a round-trip ticket to ... ... made no ōhuku kip-pu o

ichi-mai
route rūto; **what's the best route?** dore ga ichi-ban' ī rūto dess ka?
rowboat, rowing boat bōto
rubber (*material*) gom; (*eraser*) keshi-gom
rubber band wa-gom
rubbish (*waste*) gomi; (*poor quality goods*) garakta; **that's rubbish!** (*nonsense*) bakabakashī!
rucksack ryuk-k sak-k
rude busahō (na); **he was very rude** kare wa totemo busahō deshta
rug shki-mono
ruins iseki
rum ram-shu
rum and coke ram-shu to kōk
run (*person*) hashiru; **I go running** (*habitually*) ran-ning-gu o shi-mass; **quick, run!** isoide!; **how often do the buses run?** bass wa nam-pun'oki ni hasht-te i-mass ka?; **he's been run over** kare wa kuruma ni hikare-mashta; **I've run out of gas/petrol** gas-kets dess
rupture (*medical*) herunia
Russia Roshia
Russian (*adjective*) Roshia (no); (*person*) Roshia-jin; (*language*) Roshia-go

S

saccharine sak-karin
sad kanashī
saddle (*for bike, horse*) sadoru
safe anzen (na); **will it be safe here?** koko wa anzen deshō ka?; **is it a safe beach for swimming?** kono hama wa oyoide mo anzen dess ka?; **is it safe to drink?** nonde mo mugai dess ka?; **could you put this in your safe?** kore o kinko ni hokan shte kure-masen ka?
safety pin anzempin
sail (*noun*) ho; **can we go sailing?** yot-to ni nori-mashō ka?

sailboard (*noun*) sērubōdo
sailboarding: I like sailboarding sērubōdo ni noru no ga ski dess
sailor huna-nori
sake sake
sake bottle tok-kuri
sake cup sakazuki
salad sarada
salad dressing sarada doresh-shing-g
sale: is it for sale? uri-mono dess ka?; **it's not for sale** uri-mono ja ari-masen
sales clerk ten'in
salmon sake

salt shio
salty shio-karai; **it's too salty** shio-kara-sugi-mass
same onaji; **one the same as this** kore to onaji no; **the same again, please** onaji no o mō hitotsu onegai-shi-mass; **have a good time — same to you** tanoshinde irash-shai — anata mo; **it's all the same to me** dot-chi demo watashi ni wa onaji dess; **thanks all the same** tonikaku arigatō
samurai samurai
sand suna
sandals sandaru; **a pair of sandals** sandaru iss-sok
sandwich sandoit-chi; **a chicken sandwich** chikin sando
sandy suna (no); **a sandy beach** suna-hama
sanitary napkin/towel seiri-yō napkin
sarcastic iyami (na)
sardines iwashi
satisfactory manzok dekiru; **this is not satisfactory** kore de wa manzok deki-masen
Saturday doyōbi
sauce sōss
saucepan etski nabe
saucer uke-zara
sauna sauna
sausage sōsēji
sauté potatoes jaga-imo no sotē
save (*life*) taskeru; (*reserve*) tot-te ok; (*money*) tameru; (*avoid waste*) sets-yak suru; **he saved my life** kare ga inochi o taskete kure-mashta; **will you save my seat?** seki o tot-te oite kure-masen ka?; **I'm saving money** okane o tamete i-mass; **save electricity** denki o sets-yak shte kudasai
savo(u)ry shio-aji (no)
say: how do you say ... in Japanese? Nihon-go de ... o nan to ī-mass ka?; **what did you say?** nan to osh-shai-mashta ka?; **what did he say?** kare wa nan to ī-mashta ka?; **I said ...** watashi wa ... to ī-mashta; **he said ...** kare wa ... to ī-mashta; **I wouldn't say no** (*yes please*) hai, dewa enryo nak
scald: he's scalded himself kare wa yakedo shi-mashta

scarf skāf
scarlet mak-ka (na)
scenery keshki
scent (*perfume*) kōsui
schedule skejūru
scheduled flight teiki-bin
school gak-kō; (*university*) daigak; **I'm still at school** watashi wa mada gaksei dess
science kagak
scissors: a pair of scissors hasami
scooter (*motor scooter*) skūtā
scorching: it's really scorching (*weather*) kyō wa hontō ni teri-tske-mass ne
score: what's the score? skoa wa dō nat-te i-mass ka?
scotch (*whisky*) skot-chi
Scotch tape (*tm*) serotēp
Scotland Skot-torando
Scottish Skot-torando (no)
scrambled eggs iri-tamago
scratch (*noun*) kiz; **it's only a scratch** tada no hik-kaki kiz dess
scream (*verb*) sakebu
screen skurīn; (*Japanese paper screen*) byōbu
screw (*noun*) neji
screwdriver neji-mawashi
scroll (*hanging*) kakejik; (*rolled*) makimono
scrubbing brush (*for hands, for floors*) burash
scruffy (*appearance, person, hotel*) misuborashī
scuba diving skyūba daibing-g
sea umi; **by the sea** umibe de
sea air hama no kūki
seafood kaisambuts
seafood restaurant sakana sem-mon no restoran
seafront kaigan-zoi; **on the seafront** kaigan-zoi ni
seagull kamome
seal: personal seal hanko
search (*verb*) sagass; **I searched everywhere** dokomo-kamo sagashi-mashta
search party sōsak-tai
seashell kaigara
seasick hunayoi; **I feel seasick** hune ni yoi-mashta; **I get seasick** hune ni yō tachi dess

seaside: by the seaside kaigan de; **let's go to the seaside** umibe e iki-mashō

season kisets; **in the high season** kaki-ire doki ni; **in the low season** shimo-gare doki ni

seasoning chōmiryō

seat seki; **is this seat free?** kono seki wa aite i-mass ka?

seat belt shīto beruto; **do you have to wear a seat belt?** shitō beruto o shimerun dess ka?

sea urchin uni

seaweed kaisō

secluded hitome ni tskanai

second (adjective) ni-bam-me (no); (of time) byō; **just a second!** chot-to mat-te kudasai!; **can I have a second helping?** okawari deki-mass ka?

second class (travel) ni-tō

second-hand seko-han

secret (noun) himits

security check hoan keibi no kensa

sedative chinsei-zai

see miru; **I didn't see it** mi-masen deshta; **have you seen my husband?** shujin' o mikake-masen deshta ka?; **I saw him this morning** (met him) kesa kare ni ai-mashta; **can I see the manager?** manējā ni ai-tai no dess ga; **see you tonight!** ja komban ne!; **can I see?** chot-to misete kure-masen ka?; **oh, I see** (I understand) naruhodo; **will you see to it?** (arrange it) tehai shte kure-masen ka?

seldom met-ta ni ...-masen; **I seldom eat fish** sakana wa met-ta ni tabe-masen

self-service seruhu sābiss

Self Defence Force Ji-ei-tai

sell uru; **do you sell ...?** ... o ut-te i-mass ka?; **will you sell it to me?** ut-te kure-masen ka?

sellotape (tm) serotēp

send okuru; **I want to send this to England** kore o Igiriss ni okuri-tai dess; **I'll have to send this food back** kono shokuhin' o hempin shinakereba nari-masen

senior: Mr Jones senior toshi-ue no Jōnz-san

senior citizen otoshiyori

sensational (holiday, experience etc) sugok subarashī

sense: I have no sense of direction watashi wa hōkō-onchi dess; **it doesn't make sense** sore dewa imi ga tsūji-masen

sensible (person, idea) humbets no aru

sensitive (person, skin) binkan (na)

sentimental kanshō-teki (na)

separate bets-bets (no); **can we have separate bills?** okanjō wa bets ni shte kure-masen ka?

separated: I'm separated watashi wa bek-kyo-chū dess

separately (pay, travel) bets-bets ni

September ku-gats

septic haikets-shō (no)

serious (person) majime (na); (situation, problem) jūdai (na); (illness) hidoi; **I'm serious** honki dess yo; **you can't be serious!** son-na baka-na!; **is it serious, doctor?** hidoin deshō ka, sensei?

seriously: seriously ill jūbyō (no)

service: the service was excellent sābiss wa batsgun deshta; **could we have some service, please!** dare ka ōtai no hito wa i-masen ka?; **church service** reihai; **the car needs a service** sono kuruma ni wa teiki-tenken ga hitsyō dess

service charge (in restaurant) sābiss ryōkin

service station gasorin stando

serviette napkin

set: it's time we were setting off mō shup-pats no jikan dess

set menu teishok

settle up: can we settle up now? ima seisan shi-mashō ka?

several ikutska (no)

sew nū; **could you sew this back on?** kore o nuitskete kure-masen ka?

sex (sexual intercourse) sek-ks

sexist danson johi (no)

sexy sekshī

shade: in the shade kage ni

shadow kage

shake: let's shake hands akshu shi-mashō

shallow (water) asai

shame: what a shame! okinodok ni!

shampoo (*noun*) shampū; **can I have a shampoo and set?** shampū to set-to onegai-shi-mass

shandy, shandy-gaff shandē

share (*room*) ai-beya ni suru; (*table*) ai-seki ni suru; **let's share the cost** warikan ni shi-mashō

shark same

sharp (*knife*) surudoi; (*taste*) karai

shattered: I'm shattered (*very tired*) kuta-kuta ni nari-mashta

shave: I need a shave hige o soranakereba nari-masen; **can you give me a shave?** hige o sot-te kure-masen ka?

shaver shēbā

shaving brush hige-sori-yō burash

shaving foam shēbing-g fōm

shaving point hige-sori-yō no konsento

shaving soap hige-sori-yō sek-ken

shawl shōru

she kanojo; **is she here?** kanojo wa koko ni i-mass ka?; **is she a friend of yours?** kanojo wa anata no otomodachi dess ka?; **she's not English** kanojo wa Igiriss-jin ja ari-masen; *see page 99*

sheep hitsuji

sheet (*bed linen*) shīts; **a sheet of ...** ... o ichi-mai

shelf tana

shell kaigara

shellfish kai

sherry sherī

shingles obijō hōshin

Shinto (*noun*) Shintō; (*adjective*) Shintō (no)

Shintoism Shintō

Shinto priest kan-nushi

ship hune; **by ship** (*travel*) hune de

shirt shats

shit! kso!

shock: I got a shock (*surprise*) bik-kuri shi-mashta; **I got an electric shock from the ...** ... de kanden shisō ni nari-mashta

shock-absorber shok-ku abusōbā

shocking (*behaviour, prices, custom etc*) hidoi

shoe kuts; **my shoes** watashi no kuts; **a pair of shoes** kutsu iss-sok

shoelaces kuts-himo

shoe polish kutsuzumi

shop mise

shopping: I'm going shopping kaimono ni iki-mass

shop window uindō

shore (*of sea, lake*) kishibe

short (*person*) se no hikui; (*time, journey*) mijikai; **it's only a short distance** sugu chikak dess

short-change: you've short-changed me otsuri ga tari-masen

short circuit shōto

shortcut chikamichi

shorts (*also underwear*) pants

should: what should I do? do shtara ī desho?; **he shouldn't be long** nagaku wa kakaranai haz dess; **you should have told me** oshiete kurereba yokat-ta no ni

shoulder kata

shoulder blade kenkōkots

shout (*verb*) sakebu

show: could you show me? misete kure-masen ka?; **does it show?** miete-mass ka?; **we'd like to go to a show** shō o mi-ni iki-tai dess

shower (*in bathroom*) shawā; **with shower** shawā-tski (no)

showercap shawā kyap-p

show-off: don't be a show-off kak-kō tske-naide

shrimps kuruma-ebi

shrine jinja

shrink chijimu; **it's shrunk** chijinde shimai-mashta

shut (*verb*) shimeru; **when do you shut?** koko wa its shimari-mass ka?; **when do they shut?** soko wa its shimari-mass ka?; **it was shut** shimat-te i-mashta; **I've shut myself out** jibun' o shime-dashte shimai-mashta; **shut up!** damare!

shutter (*on camera*) shat-tā; (*on window*) amado

shy hazkashi-gari (no)

sick (*ill*) byōki (no); **I think I'm going to be sick** (*vomit*) dōmo modoshi-sō na kibun dess

side yoko; (*in game*) chīm; **at the side of the road** dōro no yoko de; **the other side of town** machi no hantai-gawa

side salad soemono no sarada

side street wakimichi
sidewalk hodō
siesta hirune
sight: the sights of ... ... no kembuts
sightseeing: sightseeing tour kankō
ryokō; **we're going sightseeing**
kembuts ni dekakeru tsmori dess
sign (*roadsign etc*) hyōshki; (*written
character*) kanji; **where do I sign?**
doko ni sain shi-mashō ka?
signal: he didn't give a signal (*driver,
cyclist*) kare wa hōkō shiji shi-masen
deshta
signature shomei
signpost dōro hyōshki
silence shizkesa
silencer sairensā
silk kinu
silkworm kaiko
silly (*person, thing to do etc*) baka (na);
that's silly bakagete i-mass
silver (*noun*) gin; (*adjective*) gin (no)
silver foil gim-pak
similar onaji yō (na)
simple (*easy*) kantan (na)
since kara; **since yesterday** kinō
kara; **since we got here** koko ni
tsuite kara
sincere seijits (na)
sing utau
Singapore Shin-gapōru
singer kashu
single: a single room shin-guru beya;
a single to ... ... made katamichi
kip-pu o ichi-mai; **I'm single** watashi
wa dokshin dess
sink (*in kitchen*) nagashi; **it sank**
shizumi-mashta
sir (*to a teacher, leader etc*) sensei;
excuse me, sir shitsurei dess ga
sirloin sāroin
sister: your elder sister onē-san;
your younger sister imōto-san; **my
elder sister** ane; **my younger sister**
imōto
sister-in-law (*elder*) giri no onē-san;
my elder sister-in-law giri no ane;
(*younger*) giri no imōto-san; **my
younger sister-in-law** giri no imōto
sit suwaru; **may I sit here?** koko ni
suwat-te mo ī dess ka?; **someone is
sitting here** koko wa husagat-te i-
mass

situation jijō
size saiz; **do you have any other
sizes?** hoka no saiz wa ari-masen ka?
sketch (*noun*) sket-chi
ski (*noun*) skī; (*verb*) skī o suru
ski boots skī guts
skid: I skidded yoko-suberi shi-
mashta
skin hihu
skin-diving skin-daibing-g
skinny yaseta
skirt skāto
skull zugaikots
sky sora
skyscraper kōsōbiru
sleep nemuru; **I can't sleep** nemure-
masen; **did you sleep well?** yok
nemure-mashta ka?; **I need a good
sleep** jūbun na suimin' o tori-tai
dess
sleeper (*rail*) shindai-sha
sleeping car (*rail*) shindai-sha
sleeping pill suimin'yak
sleepy (*person*) nemui; (*weather, day*)
mono-ui; (*town*) shizka (na); **I'm
feeling sleepy** nemuk nari-mashta
sleeve sode
slice: three slices of bread pan sam-
mai
slide (*photograph*) suraido
sliding door (*made of very thick paper*)
husuma; (*made of thinner paper*) shōji
slim (*adjective*) hoss-sori shta; **I'm
slimming** watashi wa genryō shte i-
mass
slip (*under dress*) surip-p; **I slipped**
(*on pavement etc*) suberi-mashta
slipped disc gik-kuri goshi
slippers surip-pa
slippery suberi-yasui; **it's slippery**
suberi-yasui dess
slow noroi; **slow down!** (*driving,
speaking*) mot-to yuk-kuri!
slowly yuk-kuri; **could you say it
slowly?** mot-to yuk-kuri it-te kure-
masen ka?; **very slowly** totemo yuk-
kuri
small chīsai
small change komakai-no
smallpox ten-nentō
smart (*clothes*) sumāto (na)
smashing (*holiday, time, food etc*)
subarashī

smell nioi; **there's a funny smell** hen-na nioi ga shi-mass; **what a lovely smell!** ī nioi dess nē; **it smells** (smells bad) iya na nioi ga shi-mass

smile (verb) hoho-emu

smoke (noun) kemuri; **do you smoke?** tabako o sui-mass ka?; **do you mind if I smoke?** tabako o sut-te mo kamai-masen ka?; **I don't smoke** tabako wa sui-masen

smooth (surface) nameraka (na)

snack: I'd just like a snack keishoku ga tabe-tai dess

snackbar snak-k

snake hebi

sneakers undō-guts

snob zokubuts

snorkel shunōkeru

snow (noun) yuki

so: it's so hot totemo atsui dess; **it was so beautiful!** totemo kirei deshta; **not so fast** son-na ni hayak shinaide; **thank you so much** hontō ni arigatō; **it wasn't — it was so!** sō ja ari-masen — īe sō dess yo; **so am I** watashi mo sō dess; **so do I** watashi mo sō dess; **how was it? — so-so** dō deshta ka? — mā-mā dess

soaked: I'm soaked watashi wa zubunure dess

soaking solution (for contact lenses) hozon'eki

soap sek-ken

soap-powder kona-sek-ken

sober (not drunk) shirahu (no)

soccer sak-kā

sock sok-ks

socket (electrical) soket-to

soda (water) sōda-sui

sofa sofā

soft (material etc) yawarakai

soft drink sohuto dorink

soft lenses sohuto renz

soldier heitai

sole (of shoe) kuts no soko; (of foot) ashi no ura; **could you put new soles on these?** kuts no soko o hari-kaete kure-masen ka?

solid katai

some: may I have some water? mizu o itadake-mass ka?; **do you have some matches?** mat-chi ga ari-mass ka?; **that's some drink!** are wa sugoi nomimono dess!; **some of them** (people) nan-nin ka; (things) ikuts ka; **can I have some?** skoshi itadake-mass ka?

somebody, someone dare ka

something nani ka; **something to drink** nani ka nomimono

sometime its ka; **sometime this afternoon** kyō no gogo its ka

sometimes tokidoki

somewhere doko ka

son musko-san; **my son** musko

song uta

son-in-law giri no musko-san; **my son-in-law** musume-muko

soon sugu; **I'll be back soon** sugu modot-te ki-mass; **as soon as you can** dekiru dake hayak

sore: it's sore itai dess

sore throat: I have a sore throat nodo ga itai dess

sorry: (I'm) sorry sumi-masen; **sorry?** (didn't understand) nanto osh-shai-mashta ka?

sort shurui; **a different sort of ...** chigat-ta shurui no ...; **what sort of ...?** dono yō na ...?; **will you sort it out?** umak tori-hakarat-te kure-masen ka?

soup sūp

sour (taste) sup-pai

south minami; **to the south** minami no hō e

South Africa Minami Ahurika

South African (adjective) Minami Ahurika (no); (person) Minami Ahurika-jin

southeast nantō; **to the southeast** nantō no hō e

southwest nansei; **to the southwest** nansei no hō e

souvenir omiyage

spa onsen

space heater dambō-ki

spade shaberu

spanner spana

spare part yobi no buhin

spare tyre/tire yobi no taiya

spark(ing) plug spāk purag

speak hanass; **do you speak English?** Eigo ga wakari-mass ka?; **I don't speak ... ...** wa wakari-masen; **can I**

speak to ...? ... to hanash-tai no dess ga; **this is Mr. Smith speaking** (*on telephone*) Smiss dess ga
special tokubets (na); **nothing special** hutsū no
specialist sem-mon-ka
special(i)ty sem-mon; **the special(i)ty of the house** kono mise no jiman ryōri
spectacles megane
speed (*noun*) sokudo; **he was speeding** kare wa spīdo ihan' o shte i-mashta
speedboat spīdobōto
speed limit sokudo seigen
speedometer sokudo no mētā
spell tsuzuru; **how do you spell it?** dō tsuzuri-mass ka?
spend tskau; **I've spent all my money** ari-gane o zembu tskai-hatashi-mashta
spice spaiss
spicy: it's very spicy spaiss ga yoku kīte i-mass
spider kumo
spin-dryer dass-sui-ki
splendid (*very good*) subarashī
splint (*for broken limb*) so-egi
splinter (*in finger*) toge
splitting: I've got a splitting headache atama ga wareru yō ni itami-mass
spoke (*in wheel*) spōk
sponge sponji
spoon spūn
sport spōts
sport(s) jacket spōts jaket-to
spot (*on face etc*) shimi; **will they do it on the spot?** sugu yat-te kureru deshō ka?
sprain kujik; **I've sprained my ... ...** o kujiki-mashta
spray (*for hair*) spurē
spring (*season*) haru; (*of car, seat*) spuring-g
square (*in town*) hiroba; **ten square metres** jū heihō mētoru
squash (*sport*) skash
stain (*noun: on clothes*) yogore
stairs kaidan
stale (*bread, taste*) hurui
stall: the engine keeps stalling enjin ga tomat-te bakari i-mass

stamp (*noun*) kit-te; **a stamp for England, please** Igiriss made no kit-te o kudasai
stand: I can't stand ... (*can't tolerate*) ... niwa gaman ga deki-masen
standard (*adjective*) hyōjun (no)
standby kūsekimachi
star hoshi; (*movie star*) stā
start (*noun*) stāto; **when does the film start?** eiga wa nan-ji ni hajimari-mass ka?; **the car won't start** kuruma no enjin ga kakari-masen
starter (*of car*) shidōki; (*food*) zensai
starving: I'm starving onaka ga peko-peko dess
state (*in country*) shū; (*in Japan*) ken; **the States** (*USA*) Gash-shūkok
station eki
statue chōzō
stay taizai; **we enjoyed our stay** taizai-chū wa tanoshku sugoshi-mashta; **where are you staying?** doko ni tomat-te i-mass ka?; **I'm staying at ... ...** ni tomat-te i-mass; **I'd like to stay another week** mō ish-shūkan tomari-tai dess; **I'm staying in tonight** komban wa gaishuts shi-masen
steak stēki
steal nusumu; **my bag has been stolen** watashi wa bag-gu o torare-mashta
steep (*hill*) kyū (na)
steering stearing-g; **the steering is slack** stearing-g ga amai
steering wheel kumura no handoru
step (*in front of house etc*) kaidan
stereo stereo
sterling (*currency*) eika-pondo
stew shchū
steward (*on plane*) schuādo
stewardess schuādess
sticking plaster bansōkō
sticky: it's sticky beta-beta shi-mass
sticky tape set-chak tēp
still: I'm still waiting mada mat-te i-mass; **will you still be open?** mada sono toki made aite i-mass ka?; **it's still not right** mada okashī dess; **that's still better** sono hō ga mot-to ī dess; **keep still!** ugokanaide kudasai!
sting (*by insect*) mush-sasare; **I've been**

stung nani ka ni sasare-mashta

stink (*noun*) akshū; **it stinks** hidoi nioi ga shi-mass

stockings stok-king-g

stolen nusumareta; **my wallet's been stolen** saihu ga nusumare-mashta

stomach onaka; **do you have something for an upset stomach?** shōka-huryō ni kik mono ga ari-masen ka?

stomach-ache huk-tsū

stone (*rock*) ishi; *see page 120*

stop (*bus stop*) teiryū-jo; **which is the stop for ...?** ... iki no teiryū-jo wa doko dess ka?; **please, stop here** (*to taxi driver etc*) koko de tomete kure-masen ka?; **do you stop near ...?** ... no chikak de tomari-mass ka?; **stop doing that!** yamete kudasai

stopover ryokō no kyūkei

store (*shop*) mise

stor(e)y (*of building*) ...-kai; **first storey (UK)/second story (USA)** ni-kai

storm arashi

story (*tale*) hanashi

stove stōb

straight (*road etc*) mass-sugu (na); **it's straight ahead** mass-sugu it-ta tokoro dess; **straight away** sugu; **a straight whisky** uiskī no storēto

straighten: can you straighten things out? (*sort things our*) umak naoshte kure-masen ka?

strange (*odd*) hen (na); (*unknown*) mita koto no nai

stranger mishiranu hito; **I'm a stranger here** koko wa hajimete dess

strap (*on watch*) bando; (*on dress, suitcase*) storap-p

strawberry ichigo

straw mat tatami

streak: could you put streaks in? (*in hair*) storīku o irete kure-masen ka?

stream nagare

street tōri; **on the street** tōri de; **the shop across the street** tōri no mukōgawa no mise; **cross the street** tōri o yokogiru; **in a back street** uradōri ni; **the next street** tsugi no tōri; **which street is it on?** dono tōri ni ari-mass ka?

streetcar shigai densha

streetmap dōro-chiz

strep throat itai nodo

strike: they're on strike karera wa sto-chū dess

string himo; **have you got some string?** himo ga ari-mass ka?

striped shima-moyō (no)

striptease storip-p

stroke nōsot-chū; **he's had a stroke** kare wa sot-chū no hos-sa o okoshi-mashta

stroll: let's go for a stroll sampo ni iki-mashō

stroller (*for babies*) bebī-kā

strong (*person, taste, drink, curry*) tsyoi

stuck tskaeta; **the key's stuck** kagi ga tskaete shimai-mashta

student gaksei

stupid baka (na); **that's stupid** baka rashī dess

sty(e) (*in eye*) mono-morai

subtitles jimak; **does it have subtitles?** jimakutski dess ka?

suburb kōgai

subway (*underground*) chikatets

successful: were you successful? umaku iki-mashta ka?

suddenly totsuzen ni

sue: I intend to sue ut-taeru tsmori dess

suede suēdo

sugar satō

suggest: what do you suggest? ī kan-gae ga ari-mass ka?

suit (*noun*) sūts; **it doesn't suit me** (*clothes etc*) watashi ni wa niai-masen; **it suits you** (*clothes etc*) yok niai-mass; **that suits me fine** (*arrangements*) watashi wa sore de kek-kō dess

suitable (*time, place*) tsugō no ī

suitcase sūts-kēss

sulk: he's sulking kare wa hukigen dess

sultry (*weather, climate*) hidok mushi-atsui

summer nats; **in the summer** nats ni

summer festival dance bon'odori

summer kimono yukata

sun taiyō; **in the sun** hinata de; **out of the sun** hikage de; **I've had too much sun** hi ni atari-sugi-mashta

sunbathe nik-kō yok

sunblock (*cream*) hiyake-dome

sunburn hiyake

sunburnt hi ni yaketa
Sunday nichiyōbi
sunglasses san-gurass
sunny: if it's sunny tenki ga yokereba; **a sunny day** yok hareta hi
sunrise hinode
sun roof (*in car*) san rūf
sunset nichibots
sunshade hiyoke
sunshine nik-kō
sunstroke nish-sha-byō
suntan hiyake
suntan lotion santan rōshon
suntanned hi ni yaketa
suntan oil santan' oiru
super (*time, holiday, person*) sugoi; **super!** sugoi!
superb (*buildings, sunsets, view*) batsgun (na)
supermarket sūpā
supper yūshok
supplement (*extra charge*) tsuika ryōkin
suppose: I suppose so sō kamo shire-masen
suppository za-yak
sure: I'm sure kit-to sō deshō; **are you sure?** tashka ni sō dess ka?; **he's sure** kare wa kit-to sō da to it-te i-mass; **sure!** mochiron!
surname myōji
surprise (*noun*) odoroki
surprising: that's not surprising son-na koto darō to omot-te i-mashta
suspension (*of car*) saspenshon

sutra okyō
swallow (*verb*) nomikomu
swearword gehin na kotoba
sweat (*verb*) ase o kak; (*noun*) ase; **I'm covered in sweat** ase bish-shori ni nat-te i-mass
sweater sētā
sweatshirt suet-to shāts
sweet (*taste*) amai; (*noun, dessert*) dezāto
sweet and sour pork subuta
sweets ame
swelling hare
sweltering: it's sweltering udari-mass ne
swerve: I had to swerve (*when driving*) kyū-handoru o kiranakereba nari-masen deshta
swim (*verb*) oyogu; **I'm going for a swim** oyogi ni iki-mass; **do you want to go for a swim?** oyogi ni iki-tai dess ka?; **I can't swim** watashi wa oyoge-masen
swimming suiei; **I like swimming** watashi wa suiei ga ski dess
swimming costume suiei-gi
swimming pool pūru
swimming trunks suiei-pants
switch (*noun*) suit-chi; **could you switch it on?** tskete kure-masen ka?; **could you switch it off?** keshte kure-masen ka?
swollen hare-agat-ta
swollen glands hare-agat-ta sen
sympathy dōjō
synagogue yudaya-kyō no reihaidō
synthetic gōsei (no)

T

table tēburu; **a table for two** hutari-yō no tēburu; **at our usual table** itsmo no tēburu de.
tablecloth tēburu-kuross
table tennis tak-kyū; **shall we play table tennis?** tak-kyū o shi-mashō ka?

tactful (*person*) josainai
tailback (*of traffic*) kuruma no rets
tailor shtate-ya
Taiwan Taiwan
Taiwanese (*adjective*) Taiwan (no); (*person*) Taiwan-jin
take: will you take this to room 12?

kore o jūni-gō-shits ni todokete kure-masen ka?; **will you take me to the airport?** watashi o kūkō made tsurete it-te kure-masen ka?; **do you take credit cards?** kurejit-to kādo demo ī dess ka?; **OK, I'll take it** ja sore ni shiyō; **how long does it take?** dono kurai jikan ga kakari-mass ka?; **it'll take 2 hours** ni-jikan hodo kakari-mass; **I can't take too much sun** amari taiyō ni wa tsyoku ari-masen; **to take away please** (hamburger etc) mochi-kaeri yō ni shte kudasai; **will you take this back, it's broken** kore wa hempin shi-mass, kowarete ita node; **could you take it in at the side?** (dress, jacket) kore no waki o tsmete kure-masen ka?; **when does the plane take off?** hikōki wa its shup-pats shi-mass ka?; **can you take a little off the top?** (to hair-dresser) ue no hō o skoshi kit-te kure-masen ka?

talcum powder tarukamu paudā
talk (verb) hanass
tall (person) se ga takai; (building) takai
tampax (tm) tampak-ks
tampons tampon
tan (noun) hiyake; **I want to get a good tan** yok hi ni yake-tai dess
tank (of car) nenryō tank
tap (for water) jaguchi; (for gas, on barrel) sen
tape (for cassette) tēp; (sticky) serotēp
tape measure maki-jak
tape recorder tēpu rekōdā
taste (noun) aji; **can I taste it?** aji-mi shte ī dess ka?; **it has a peculiar taste** kawat-ta aji ga shi-mass; **it tastes very nice** totemo oishī dess; **it tastes revolting** hidoi aji dess
taxi takshī; **will you get me a taxi?** takshī o yonde kure-masen ka?
taxi driver takshī no untenshu
taxi rank, taxi stand takshī noriba
tea: black tea kōcha; **green/Japanese tea** ocha; **tea with milk** miruk tī; **tea for two please** kōcha o hutari-bun' onegai-shi-mass; **could I have a cup of tea?** kōcha o ip-pai itadake-masen ka?
teabag tībag-g
tea ceremony chanoyu

teach oshieru; **could you teach me?** watashi ni oshiete kure-masen ka?; **could you teach me Japanese?** Nihon-go o oshiete kure-masen ka?
teacher sensei
tea house chamise
team chīm
teapot (for green tea) kyūss; (for black tea) pot-to
tea towel hukin
teenager tīn'eijā
teetotal: he's teetotal kare wa zet-tai ni sake o nomi-masen
telegram dempō; **I want to send a telegram** dempō o uchi-tai no dess
telephone denwa; **can I make a telephone call?** denwa o kake-sasete kure-masen ka?; **could you talk to him for me on the telephone?** watashi no kawari ni denwa shte kure-masen ka?
telephone box/booth denwa bok-ks
telephone directory denwa-chō
telephone number denwa ban-gō; **what's your telephone number?** otak no denwa ban-gō wa namban dess ka?
telephoto lens bōen renz
television terebi; **I'd like to watch television** terebi ga mi-tai dess; **is the match on television?** terebi de shiai o hōei shte i-mass ka?
tell: could you tell him that I called? (on telephone) watashi ga denwa shta to kare ni tstaete kure-masen ka?; (visited) watashi ga kita to kare ni tstaete kure-masen ka?
temperature (weather) ki-on; (of body) tai-on; (fever) nets; **he has a temperature** kare wa nets ga ari-mass
temple (religious) otera
temporary kari (no)
tenant (of apartment) kyojūsha
tennis teniss
tennis ball teniss bōru
tennis court teniss kōto; **can we use the tennis court?** teniss kōto o tskat-te mo ī dess ka?
tennis racket teniss raket-to
tent tento
term (at university, school) gak-ki
terminus (rail) shūten

terrace terass; **on the terrace** terass
de
terrible (*weather, food, accent*) hidoi
terrific (*weather, food, teacher*) totemo ī
testicle kōgan
than yorimo; **smaller then ... ...**
yorimo chīsai
thanks, thank you arigatō; **thank you
very much** hontō ni arigatō gozai-
mass; **thank you for everything** iro-
íro to arigatō gozai-mashta; **no
thanks** īe kek-kō dess
that: that woman ano josei; **that man**
ano dansei; **that one** are; **I hope
that ... ...**-tara ī dess nē; **I hope that
the shops are open** mise ga aite i-
tara ī dess ne; **that's perfect** sore de
pit-tari dess; **that's strange** sore wa
hen dess ne; **is that ...?** sore wa ...
dess ka?; **that's it** (*that's right*) sono
tōri dess; **is it that expensive?** son-
na ni takai dess ka?; *see pages 101,
113*
the *see page 99*
theatre, theater geki-jō
their (*of people*) karera no; **their
house** karera no ie; *see page 113*
theirs karera no; *see page 101*
them (*male*) karera; (*female*)
kanojotachi; (*things*) kore; **for them**
karera no tame ni; **with them** karera
to ish-sho ni; **I gave it to them**
karera ni age-mashta; **who? —
them** dare dess ka? — karera dess;
see page 100
then sorekara
there soko de; **over there** mukō ni;
up there asoko ni; **is there ...?** ... ga
ari-mass ka?; **are there ...?** ... ga ari-
mass ka?; **there is ... ...** ga ari-mass;
there are ... ... ga ari-mass; **there
you are** (*giving something*) dōzo
thermal spring onsen
thermometer (*for weather*) kandan-kei;
(*medical*) tai-on-kei; (*other*) ondo-kei
thermos flask mahō-bin
thermostat (*in car*) sāmostat-to
these kore; **can I have these?** kore o
morat-te mo ī dess ka?
they (*male*) karera; (*female*)
kanojotachi; (*objects*) sorera; **are they
ready?** yōi ga deki-mashta ka?; **are
they coming?** kuru tsmori dess ka?;

see page 99
thick atsui; (*stupid*) atama no nibui
thief koso-doro
thigh momo
thin (*people*) yaseta; (*objects*) usui
thing mono; **have you seen my
things?** watashi no mochimono c
mi-kake-masen deshta ka?; **first
thing in the morning** asa maz daīchi
ni
think kan-gaeru; **what do you think?**
anata wa dō omoi-mass ka?; **I think
so** watashi wa sō omoi-mass; **I don't
think so** watashi wa sō omoi-masen;
I'll think about it sono koto ni tsuite
wa kan-gaete oki-mass
third party insurance daisan-sha
hoken
thirsty nodo ga kawaita; **I'm thirsty**
nodo ga kawaki-mashta
this: this hotel kono hoteru; **this
street** kono tōri; **this one** kore; **this
is ...** kochira wa ... dess; **this is my
wife** kore wa kanai dess; **this is my
favo(u)rite café** kore wa watashi no
ki-ni-iri no kiss-saten dess; **is this
yours?** kore wa anata no dess ka?
those are; **not these, those** kore ja
naku, are dess; *see pages 101, 113*
thread (*noun*) ito
throat nodo
throat lozenges torōchi
throttle (*on motorbike*) surot-toru
through: through ... ... o tōt-te; **does
it go through Kyoto?** Kyōto o tōri-
mass ka?; **Monday through Friday**
getsyōbi kara kin'yōbi made; **straight
through the city centre** machi no
naka o mass-sugu tōri-nukete
through train choktsū resh-sha
throw (*verb*) nageru; **don't throw it
away** stenaide kudasai; **I'm going to
throw up** (*be sick*) haki-dashi sō dess
thumb oya-yubi
thumbtack gabyō
thunder (*noun*) kaminari
thunderstorm rai-u
Thursday mokuyōbi
ticket (*for bus, train, plane, cinema,
cloakroom*) kip-p
ticket office (*bus, rail*) kip-pu uriba
tie (*noun: around neck*) nektai
tight (*clothes etc*) kitsui; **the waist is**

too tight uesto ga kitsu-sugi-mass
tights taits
time jikan; **what's the time?** ima
nan-ji dess ka?; **at what time do you
close?** nan-ji ni shime-mass ka?;
there's not much time amari jikan
ga ari-masen; **for the time being**
sashi-atari; **from time to time**
tokidoki; **right on time** jikan dōri;
this time konkai; **last time** senkai;
next time kondo; **four times**
yon-kai; **four times as large as ... ...**
no yom-bai mo ōkī; **have a good
time!** tanoshku sugoshte kudasai; *see
page 117*
timetable (*transport*) jikok-hyō; (*plan*)
yotei-hyō
tin (*can*) kan
tinfoil arumi-hoiru
tin-opener kan-kiri
tiny totemo chīsai
tip (*for waiter etc*) chip-p; **does that include the tip?** sore ni wa chip-p mo
hukumarete i-mass ka?
tire (*for car*) taiya
tired tskareta; **I'm tired** tskare-mashta
tiring tskareru
tissues tish-shū
to: to ... ... e; **to London** Rondon' e;
to the airport kūkō e; **here's to you!**
(*toast*) anata no tame ni kampai!; *see
page 117*
toast (*bread*) tōsto; (*drinking*) kampai;
let's have a toast kampai shi-mashō
tobacco tabako
tobacconist, tobacco store tabako-ya
today kyō; **today week** raishū no kyō
toe tsmasaki
toffee kyarameru
together ish-sho ni; **we're together**
watashtachi wa ish-sho dess; **can we
pay together?** ish-sho ni harai-mashō
ka?
toilet otearai; **where's the toilet?**
otearai wa doko dess ka?; **I have to
go to the toilet** otearai ni iki-tai no
dess ga; **she's in the toilet** kanojo
wa otearai ni i-mass
toilet paper toiret-to pēpā
toilet water koron-sui
toll (*for motorway, bridge etc*) ryōkin
tomato tomato
tomato juice tomato jūss

tomato ketchup kechap-p
tomorrow ashta; **tomorrow morning**
ashta no asa; **tomorrow afternoon**
ashta no gogo; **tomorrow evening**
ashta no yoru; **the day after
tomorrow** asat-te; **see you tomorrow**
ja mata ashta
ton ton; *see page 120*
toner (*cosmetic*) tōnā
tongue shta
tonic (water) tonik-k
tonight komban; **not tonight** komban
wa dame dess
tonsillitis hentōsen'en
tonsils hentōsen
too: too ... (*excessively*) ...-sugi-mass;
(*also*) mo; **too hot** atsu-sugi-mass; **too
much** ō-sugi-mass; **me too** watashi
mo; **I'm not feeling too good** kibun
ga amari yoku ari-masen
tooth ha
toothache ha-ita
toothbrush ha-burash
toothpaste ha-migaki
top: on top of ... ... no ue ni; **on top
of the car** kuruma no ue ni; **on the
top floor** saijō-kai ni; **at the top** tep-
pen ni; **at the top of the hill** oka no
tep-pen ni; **top quality** saikō no
hinshits; **bikini top** bikini top-p
topless top-puress
torch kaichū dentō
total (*noun*) gōkei
touch (*verb*) sawaru; **let's keep in
touch** renraku o tori-ai-mashō
tough (*meat*) katai; **tough luck!** zan-
nen deshta ne
tour (*noun*) tsuā; **is there a tour of
...?** ... no tsuā ga ari-mass ka?
tour guide gaido
tourist ryokō-sha
tourist information office kankō
an-naisho
touristy: somewhere not so touristy
doko ka kankō-zure shte inai tokoro
tow: can you give me a tow? kuruma
o ken'in shte kure-masen ka?
toward(s): toward(s) ... ... no hō e
towel taoru
town machi; **in town** machi de;
which bus goes into town? machi e
ik no wa dono bass dess ka?; **we're
staying just out of town** machi no

hazure ni tomat-te i-mass
town hall (*administrative*) shiyaksho;
(*for concerts etc*) kōkaidō
tow rope ken'in rōp
toy omocha
track suit torak-k sūts
trade fair buss-san-ten
traditional dentō-teki (na); **a traditional Japanese meal** dentō-teki na
wahū ryōri
traffic kōtsū
traffic cop kōtsū junshi-in
traffic jam kōtsū no konzats
traffic light(s) shin-gō
trailer (*for carrying tent etc*) torērā
train densha; **when's the next train
to ...?** ... iki no tsugi no densha wa
nan-ji hats dess ka?; **by train** densha
de
trainers (*shoes*) torēning-g shūz
train station eki
tram shigai densha
tramp (*person*) hurōsha
tranquillizers torankiraizā
transfer desk noritsugi an-nai
transformer (*electrical*) hen'ats-ki
transitor (radio) toranjistā
transit lounge (*at airport*) noritsugi-yō
machiai-shits
translate hon'yak suru; **could you
translate that?** sore o hon'yak shte
kure-masen ka?
translation hon'yak
translator hon'yak-sha
transmission (*of car*) toransmish-shon
travel ryokō suru; **we're travel(l)ing
around** achi-kochi o ryokō shte i-
mass
travel agent ryokō gaisha
travel(l)er ryokō-sha
traveller's cheque, traveler's check
toraberāz chek-k
tray obon
tree ki
tremendous totemo ōki
trendy (*person, clothes, restaurant*)
saishin ryūkō (no)
tricky (*difficult*) muzukashī
trim: just a trim please (*to hairdresser*)
ke-saki o soroeru teido ni onegai-
shi-mass
trip (*journey*) tabi; **I'd like to go on a
trip to ...** ... e tabi ni de-tai dess;

have a good trip! yoi goryokō o!
tripod (*for camera*) sankyak
tropical (*heat, climate*) net-tai (no)
trouble (*noun*) yak-kai goto; **I'm having trouble with ...** ... de komat-te
iru koto ga ari-mass; **sorry to
trouble you** gomendō o kakete
sumi-masen
trousers zubon
trouser suit surak-ks sūts
trout mass
truck torak-k
truck driver torak-k no untenshu
true hontō (no); **that's not true** sore
wa hontō ja ari-masen
trunk kuruma no torank; (*for belongings: big case*) torank
trunks (*swimming*) suiei pants
truth hontō; **it's the truth** sore ga
hontō dess
try tamess; **please try** dōzo tameshte
mite kudasai; **will you try for me?**
chot-to yat-te mite kure-masen ka?;
I've never tried it (*food etc*) mada
ichi-do mo tameshta koto ga ari-
masen; **can I have a try?** (*food, at
doing something*) tameshte mite ī dess
ka?; **may I try it on?** (*clothes*) shichak
shte ī dess ka?
T-shirt tī shats
tube (*for tyre*) chūb
Tuesday kayōbi
tuition kyōju; **I'd like tuition**
osowari-tai dess
tulip chūrip-p
tuna fish maguro
tune (*noun*) senrits
tunnel ton-neru
turn: it's my turn now watashi no
ban dess; **turn left** hidari e magat-te
kudasai; **where do we turn off?**
doko de magari-mass ka?; **can you
turn the air-conditioning on?** eya-
kon' o tskete kure-masen ka?; **can
you turn the air-conditioning off?**
eya-kon' o keshte kure-masen ka?;
he didn't turn up kare wa ki-masen
deshta
turning (*in road*) magari-kado
TV terebi
tweezers kenuki
twice ni-kai; **twice as much** ni-bai
twin beds tsuin bed-do

twin room tsuin no heya
twins hutago
twist: I've twisted my ankle ashkubi
  o kujiki-mashta
type (*noun*) shurui; **a different type
  of ...** bets no shurui no ...
typewriter taipuraitā

typhoid chōchihuss
typhoon taihū
typical (*dish etc*) daihyō-teki (na);
  that's typical! yoku aru koto dess
  ne!
tyre taiya

U

ugly (*person, building*) minikui
ulcer kaiyō
Ulster Arustā
umbrella kasa
uncle oji-san; **my uncle** oji
uncomfortable (*chair etc*) kokochi ga
  yok nai
unconscious mu-ishki (na)
under (*spatially*) shta; (*less than*) ika;
  (*in dictionary, telephone directory*) kō; **I
  left my coat under the seat** seki no
  shta ni kōto o oki-wasure-mashta;
  Nakamura-ya is under confectioners
  Nakamura-ya wa kashi-ya no kō ni
  ari-mass
underdone (*meat*) nama yake (no)
undergraduate daigaksei
underground (*rail*) chikatets
underpants pants
undershirt shats
understand wakaru; **I don't understand** wakari-masen; **I understand**
  wakari-mass; **do you understand?**
  wakari-mass ka?
underwear shtagi
undo (*clothes*) hazuss
uneatable taberarenai; **it's uneatable**
  sore wa taberare-masen
unemployed shitsgyō-chū
unfair hukōhei (na); **that's unfair**
  sore wa hukōhei dess
unfortunately zan-nen-nagara
unfriendly yoso-yososhī
unhappy kanashī
unhealthy (*person, climate etc*) hukenkō
  (na)
United Nations Kokuren

United States Gash-shūkok; **in the
  United States** Gash-shūkok de
university daigak
unlimited mileage (*on hire car*)
  museigen na sōkō-kyori
unlock kagi o akeru; **the door was
  unlocked** doa wa aite i-mashta
unpack nihodoki suru
unpleasant (*person, taste*) huyukai (na)
untie tok
until made; **until we meet again** (*said
  as parting words*) ja mata; **until next
  week** raishū made; **not until Wednesday** suiyōbi made wa dame dess
unusal kawat-ta
up: further up the road kono michi o
  mot-to it-ta tokoro ni; **up there**
  asoko ni; **he's not up yet** (*not out of
  bed*) kare wa mada nete i-mass;
  what's up? (*what's wrong?*) dō ka
  shi-mashta ka?
upmarket (*restaurant, hotel, goods etc*)
  kōkyū
upset stomach chōshi no okashī
  onaka
upside down sakasama
upstairs ue
urgent kinkyū (na); **it's very urgent**
  kore wa kinkyū o yōshi-mass
urinary tract infection nyōdō-en
us watashtachi; **with us** watashtachi
  to; **for us** watashtachi no tame ni;
  see page 100
use (*verb*) tskau; **may I use ...?** ... o
  tskat-te mo ī dess ka?
used: I used to swim a lot yoku
  oyoida mono dess; **when I get used**

to the heat atsusa ni naretara
useful yaku ni tats
usual hutsū (no); **as usual** itsmo no
tōri
usually hutsū wa
U-turn yū-tān

V

vacancy: do you have any vacancies?
(*hotel*) aki-beya ga ari-mass ka?
vacation kyūka; **we're here on vacation** watashtachi wa kyūka de koko e ki-mashta
vaccination yobō-chūsha
vacuum cleaner sōjiki
vacuum flask mahō-bin
vagina chits
valid (*ticket etc*) yūkō (na); **how long is it valid for?** kore wa dono kurai no kikan yūkō dess ka?
valley tani
valuable (*adjective*) kichō (na); **can I leave my valuables here?** kichō-hin' o koko ni azukete ī dess ka?
value (*noun*) kachi
van ban
vanilla banira; **a vanilla ice cream** banira aiss-kurīm
varicose veins jōmyaku ryū
variety show baraetī shō
vary: it varies bāi ni yot-te chigai-mass
vase kabin
vaudeville baraetī shō
VD seibyō
veal koushi no nik
vegetables yasai
vegetarian saishok shugisha; **I'm a vegetarian** watashi wa saishok shugi dess
velvet birōdo

vending machine jidō hambaiki
ventilator kanki-sen
very totemo; **just a very little Japanese** Nihon-go o skoshi bakari; **just a very little for me** watashi ni wa skoshi dake; **I like it very much** totemo ski dess
vest (*under shirt*) shats; (*waistcoat*) besto
via keiyu de; **via Kobe** Kōbe keiyu de
video (*noun: film*) bideo tēp; (*recorder*) bideo rekōdā
view nagame; **what a superb view!** totemo kirei na nagame dess ne!
viewfinder (*of camera*) faindā
village mura
violet (*flower*) sumire
vine budō no ki
vinegar su
visa biza
visibility (*for driving etc*) shkai
visit (*verb*) tazneru; **I'd like to visit ...** ... o tazne-tai dess; **come and visit us** watashtachi no tokoro e zehi oide kudasai
vital taisets; **it's vital that ...** ... wa totemo taisets na ten dess
vitamins bitamin
vodka uok-ka
voice koe
volcano kazan
voltage den'ats
vomit hakidass

W

wafer (*with ice cream*) uefā
waist uesto
waistcoat besto
wait mats; **wait for me** mat-te kudasai; **don't wait for me** matanaide kudasai; **it was worth waiting for** mat-ta kai ga ari-mashta; **I'll wait until my wife comes** kanai ga kuru made machi-mass; **I'll wait a little longer** mō skoshi mat-te mimass; **can you do it while I wait?** mat-te iru aida ni yat-te kure-masen ka?
waiter uētā; **waiter!** uētā-san!
waiting room machi-ai shits
waitress uētoress; **waitress!** chot-to onegai-shi-mass
wake okoss; **will you wake me up at 6.30?** roku-ji han ni okoshte kudasai
Wales Uēruz
walk aruk; **let's walk there** soko made aruki-mashō; **is it possible to walk there?** aruite ike-mass ka?; **I'll walk back** aruite kaeri-mass; **is it a long walk?** nagaku arukun dess ka?; **it's only a short walk** aruite sugu dess; **I'm going out for a walk** sampo ni dekakeru tsmori dess; **let's take a walk around town** machi no naka o aruite mi-mashō
walking: I want to do some walking skoshi aruki-mawari-tai dess
walking boots haiking-g shūz
walking stick sampo-yō no stek-ki
walkman (*tm*) uōkman
wall kabe
wallet saihu
wander: I like just wandering around sokora o bura-bura shtai dess
want: I want a ... ... ga hoshī dess; **I don't want any ... ...** wa hoshku ari-masen; **I want to go home** ie ni kaeri-tai dess; **I don't want to** sō sh-

taku ari-masen; **he wants to ...** kare wa ...-tai dess; **what do you want?** nani ga hoshī dess ka?; *see page 106*
war sensō
ward (*in hospital*) byōtō
warm atatakai; **it's so warm today** kyō wa atatakai dess ne; **I'm so warm** watashi wa atsku kanji-mass
warning (*noun*) keikok
was: it was ... ... deshta; *see page 108*
wash (*verb*) arau; **I need a wash** semmen shtai no dess ga; **can you wash the car?** sensha shte kure-masen ka?; **can you wash these?** kore o arat-te kure-masen ka?; **it'll wash off** kirei ni ochiru deshō
washcloth tenugui
washer (*for bolt etc*) wash-shā
washhand basin sem-men dai
washing (*clothes*) sentak-mono; **where can I hang my washing?** sentak-mono wa doko ni hoshtara ī dess ka?; **can you do my washing for me?** watashi no mono o sentak shte kure-masen ka?
washing machine sentaku-ki
washing powder senzai
washing-up: I'll do the washing-up watashi ga sara-arai o shi-mass
washing-up liquid shok-ki-yō senzai
wasp hachi
wasteful: that's wasteful mot-tai nai dess
wastepaper basket chiri-bako
watch (*wrist-*) tokei; **will you watch my things for me?** watashi no nimotsu o mite ite kure-masen ka?; **I'll just watch** watashi wa miru dake ni shi-mass; **watch out!** abunai!
watch strap tokei no bando
water mizu; **may I have some water?** mizu o itadake-masen ka?
watercolo(u)r suisai

waterproof (*adjective*) bōsui (no)
waterski: I'd like to learn to waterski suijō skī ga narai-tai dess
water sports uōtā spōts
wave (*in sea*) nami
way: which way is it? dot-chi no hō dess ka?; **it's this way** kot-chi no hō dess; **it's that way** at-chi no hō dess; **could you tell me the way to ...?** ... e wa dō it-tara ī dess ka?; **is it on the way to Kobe?** Kōbe e ik michi dess ka?; **you're blocking the way** michi o husaide-i-mass; **is it a long way to ...?** ... made tōi dess ka?; **would you show me the way to do it?** sono yari-kata o oshiete kure-masen ka?; **do it this way** kō shte mite kudasai; **no way!** dame dess!
we watashtachi; *see pages 99, 111*
weak (*person, drink*) yowai
wealthy yūhuku (na)
weather tenki; **what foul weather!** iya na tenki dess ne!; **what beautiful weather!** ī tenki dess ne!
weather forecast tenki yohō
wedding kek-kon shki
wedding anniversary kek-kon kinembi
wedding ring kek-kon' yubiwa
Wednesday suiyōbi
week shū; **a week (from) today** raishū no kyō; **a week (from) tomorrow** raishū no ashta; **Monday week** saraishū no getsyōbi
weekend shūmats; **at/on the weekend** shūmats ni
weight omosa; **I want to lose weight** yase-tai dess
weight limit (*for baggage, bridge*) jūryō seigen
weird (*person, custom, thing to happen*) kimyō (na)
welcome: welcome to ... ... e yoku irash-shai-mashta; **you're welcome** (*don't mention it*) dō itashi-mashte
well: I don't feel well kibun ga sugure-masen; **I haven't been very well** chot-to byōki shte i-mashta; **she's not well** kanojo wa byōki dess; **how are you — very well, thanks** gokigen' ikaga dess ka? — hai, okage-sama de; **you speak English very well** Eigo ga totemo jōz dess

ne; **me as well** watashi mo sō dess; **well done!** umai dess ne!; **well well!** (*surprise*) oya oya!
well-done (*meat*) ueru dan
wellingtons nagaguts
Welsh Uēruz (no)
were *see page 108*
west nishi; **to the west** nishi no hō e; **the West** Seiyō
Westerner Seiyō-jin
Western-style yōhū
West Indian (*adjective*) Nishi Indo (no); (*person*) Nishi Indo-jin
West Indies Nishi Indo shotō
wet nureta; **it's all wet** suk-kari nurete i-mass; **it's been wet all week** konshū wa zut-to ame deshta
wet suit (*for diving etc*) uet-to sūts
whale kujira
what? nan dess ka?; **what's that?** sore wa nan dess ka?; **what is he saying?** kare wa nan to ī-mashta ka?; **I don't know what to do** dō shtara ī ka wakari-masen; **what a view!** ī nagame dess ne!
wheel sharin
wheelchair kuruma-iss
when? its?; **when can we meet?** its oai deki-mass ka?; **when do we leave?** its de-mass ka?; **when does it leave?** its de-mass ka?; **when does it close?** its shimari-mass ka?; **when we get back** (*after*) kaet-te kara; **when we got back** (*at the time*) kaet-ta toki
where? doko dess ka?; **where is ...?** ... wa doko dess ka?; **I don't know where he is** kare ga doko ni iru no ka shiri-masen; **that's where I left it** soko ni oitan dess ga
which: which bus? dono bass dess ka?; **which one?** dore dess ka?; **which is yours?** anata no wa dot-chi dess ka?; **I forget which it was** dot-chi dat-ta ka wasure-mashta; **the one which ... ...** no
while aida ni; **while I'm here** koko ni iru aida ni
whipped cream hoip-p kurīm
whisky uiskī
whisper (*verb*) sasayak
white shiroi
white collar worker sararī-man
white wine shiro wain

who? dare dess ka?; **who was that?** are wa donata dess ka?; **the man who** ... ... hito

whole: the whole week maru ish-shūkan; **two whole days** maru hutska; **the whole lot** zembu

whooping cough hyaku-nichi zeki

whose: whose is this? kore wa dare no mono dess ka?

why? dōshte dess ka?; **why not?** dōshte dess ka?; **that's why it's not working** ugokanai gen'in wa sore dess; **why can't you?** dōshte deki-masen ka?

wide hiroi

wide-angle lens kōkak renz

widow mibōjin

widower otoko-yamome

wife ok-san; **my wife** kanai; **his wife** kare no ok-san

wig katsura

will: will you ask him? kare ni taznete kure-masen ka?; **see page 106**

willow yanagi

win (*verb*) kats; **who won?** dare ga kachi-mashta ka?

wind (*noun*) kaze

window mado; **near the window** mado no soba de; **in the window** (*of shop*) shō uindō no naka ni

window seat mado-gawa no seki

windscreen, windshield huronto garass

windscreen wipers, windshield wipers huronto garass no waipā

windsurfing uindo sāfin

windy kaze no aru; **it's so windy** kaze ga tsyoi dess

wine wain; **can we have some more wine?** wain' o mot-to onegai-shi-mass

wine glass wain gurass

wine list wain no risto

wing (*of plane, bird, car*) tsubasa

wing mirror saido mirā

winter huyu; **in the winter** huyu ni

winter holiday huyu yasumi

wire waiya; (*electrical*) kōdo

wireless rajio

wiring haisen

wish: give (him) my best wishes (kare ni) yoroshku otstae kudasai

wisteria huji

with ...to ish-sho ni; **I work with him** kare to ish-sho ni hataraite i-mass; **coffee with sugar** satō iri no kōhī; (*using*) **write with a pen** pen de kaki-mass; **I want to go with you** anata to ish-sho ni iki-tain dess; **I was with Mr. Tanaka** Tanaka-san to ish-sho deshta; **I'm staying with** ... ... no tokoro ni tomat-te i-mass

without nashi de; **coffee without sugar** satō nashi no kōhī

witness shōnin; **will you be a witness for me?** watashi no shōnin ni nat-te kudasai-masen ka?

witty kichi no aru

wobble: the wheel/the leg wobbles sharin/ashi ga gura-tsuite i-mass

woman josei

women josei

wonderful (*holiday, meal, weather, person*) subarashī

won't: it won't start dō shte mo stāto shi-masen; *see page 106*

wood (*material*) zaimok

woods (*forest*) mori

wool yōmō

word kotoba; **you have my word** yaksok shi-mass

work (*verb*) hatarak; (*noun*) shigoto; **how does it work?** dō yat-te ugok no dess ka?; **it's not working** sadō shte i-masen; **I work in an office** jimusho de hataraki-mass; **do you have any work for me?** nani ka shigoto ga ari-masen ka?; **when do you finish work?** its shigoto ga owari-mass ka?

world sekai; **all over the world** sekai-jū de

worn-out (*person*) heto-heto (na); (*shoes, clothes*) tskai-hurushi (no)

worry: I'm worried about her kanojo no koto ga shimpai dess; **don't worry** shimpai shinaide kudasai

worse: it's worse mae yori mo waruk nari-mashta; **it's getting worse** waruk naru ip-pō dess

worst sai-ak (no)

worth: it's not worth 500 yen go-hyaku en no neuchi wa ari-masen; **it's worth more than that** sore ijō no kachi ga ari-mass; **is it worth a visit?** it-te miru dake no kachi ga ari-mass ka?

would: would you give this to Mr ...? kore o ...-san ni agete kuremasen ka?; **what would you do?** anata nara dō shi-mass ka?

wrap: could you wrap it up? kore o tsutsunde kure-masen ka?

wrapping hōsō

wrapping paper hōsō-shi

wrench (*tool*) renchi

wrestler (*professional wrestler*) resurā; (*sumo wrestler*) sumōtori

wrestling (*professional wrestling*) puroress; (*Japanese wrestling*) sumō

wrist tekubi

write kak; **could you write it down?** kaki-tomete kure-masen ka?; **how do you write it?** dō kaki-mass ka?; **I'll write to you** tegami o kaki-mass; **I wrote to you last month** sen-gets otegami o dashi-mashta

write-off: it's a write-off (*car etc*) kore wa haiki-shobun dess

writer bumpitska

writing (*letter*) moji; **Japanese writing** (*way of writing*) kaki-kata; **the writing of a Chinese character** kanji no kaki-kata; **you have to apply in writing** bunsho de mōshkomanakereba nari-masen

writing paper binsen

written oracle omikuji

wrong: you're wrong anata wa machigat-te i-mass; **the bill's wrong** kanjō-gaki wa machigat-te i-mass; **sorry, wrong number** sumi-masen ban-gō o machigae-mashta; **I'm on the wrong train** machigaete kono densha ni not-te shimai-mashta; **I went to the wrong room** chigau heya e iki-mashta; **that's the wrong key** sore wa kagi ga chigat-te i-mass; **there's something wrong with ... ...** wa nani ka okashī dess; **what's wrong?** nani ka hen dess ka?; **is something wrong with it?** kore no doko ga okashī dess ka?

X

X-ray rentogen shashin

Y

yacht yot-to

yacht club yot-to kurab

yard: in the yard niwa de; *see page 119*

year toshi; **this year** kotoshi; **last year** kyonen; **next year** rainen; **every year** mainen; **one year** ichi-nen; **two years** ni-nen; **three years ago** sannen mae ni; **once a year** mainen ik-kai; **in a year's time** ato ichi-nen de; **it'll take a year** ichi-nen kakari-mass

yellow kīroi

yellow pages shokugyō-bets denwa-chō

yen en

yes hai; *see page 114*

yesterday kinō; **yesterday morning** kinō no asa; **yesterday afternoon** kinō no gogo; **the day before yesterday** ototoi

yet: has it arrived yet? mada todoki-masen ka?; **not yet** mada dess

yobbo yotamono
yog(h)urt yōguruto
you (*singular*) anata; (*plural*)
anatatachi; **this is for you** kore o
anata ni age-mass; **with you** anata to
ish-sho ni; *see page 99*
young wakai
young people wakamono

your (*singular*) anata no; (*plural*)
anatatachi no; **your camera** anata no
kamera; *see page 113*
yours (*singular*) anata no; (*plural*)
anatatachi no; *see page 101*
youth hostel yūss hosteru; **we're
youth hostel(l)ing** yūss hosteru ni
tomat-te i-mass

Z

Zen Zen
Zen Buddhism Zen
Zen garden Zen-tei
Zen priest Zen-sō
Zen sect Zen-shū
Zen temple Zen-dera

zero zero
zip, zipper fasnā; **could you put a
new zip on?** atarashī fasnā ni kaete
kure-masen ka?
zoo dōbutsu-en
zoom lens zūm renz

Japanese-English

LIST OF SUBJECT AREAS

ABBREVIATIONS

英 [*Ei*] Britain, British
中 [*Chū*] China, Chinese
仏 [*Huts*] France, French
独 [*Dok*] Germany, German
日 [*Nichi*] Japan, Japanese
JIS [*jiss*] Japan Industry Standard
電電会社 [*Denden Kaisha*]
　Japan Telegraph & Telephone
　Co. Ltd.
米 [*Bei*] USA, US
JAL [*jaru*] Japan Airlines
JAS [*jass*] Japan Agriculture and
　Forestry Standard, food
　monitoring body
JTB [*jei-tī-bī*] Japan Travel Bureau
KK [*kei-kei*] joint-stock company
NHK [*enu-echi-kei*] Japan
　Broadcasting Association
NTV [*en-tī-bī*] Nippon TV
TDA [*tī-dī-ei*] Toa Domestic
　Airlines
2DK [*ni-dī-kei*] two rooms and
　dining kitchen

AIRPORT AND PLANE

航空 [*kōkū*] airline
航空券 [*kōkū-ken*] airline ticket
空港 [*kūkō*] airport
全日空 [*Zen Nik-kū*] All Nippon
　Airways
到着 [*tōchak*] arrival(s)
搭乗口 [*tōjō-guchi*] boarding gate
搭乗券 [*tōjō-ken*] boarding pass
…行き [*... yuki*] bound for ...
バス [*bass*] bus(es)
税関 [*zeikan*] customs
出発 [*shup-pats*] departure(s)
行先 [*yuki-saki*] destination
国内線 [*kokunai-sen*] domestic
　airlines

免税店 [*menzei-ten*] duty-free shop
東口 [*higashi guchi*] east exit
ゲート [*gēto*] gate
出入国管理 [*shuts-nyū-goku-kanri*]
　immigration
案内 [*an-nai*] information
案内係 [*an-nai gakari*]
　information desk
国際線 [*koksai-sen*] international
　airlines
日本航空 [*Nihon Kōkū*]
　Japan Airlines
北口 [*kita guchi*] north exit
旅券/パスポート [*ryoken, paspōto*]
　passports
予約 [*yoyak*] reservations
南口 [*minami guchi*] south exit
タクシー [*takshī*] taxi(s)
東亞国内航空 [*Tōa Kokunai Kōkū*]
　Toa Domestic Airlines
経由 [*keiyu*] via
西口 [*nishi guchi*] west exit

BANKS

口座番号 [*kōza-ban-gō*]
　account number
外国為替公認銀行 [*gaikoku-kawase-
　kōnin-ginkō*] authorized foreign
　exchange bank
銀行 [*ginkō*] bank
両替所 [*ryōgaejo*] bureau de change,
　foreign exchange
窓口 [*madoguchi*] counter
為替レート [*kawase-rēto*]
　exchange rate
外国為替 [*gaikoku-kawase*]
　foreign exchange
為替 [*kawase*] money order
振替 [*hurikae*] transfer
旅行者小切手 [*ryokōsha-kogit-te*]
　traveller's cheque, traveler's check
円 [*en*] yen

BUSES

…行き [*... yuki*] bound for ...
バス [*bass*] bus
バス乗り場 [*bass-noriba*]
  bus boarding point
バスセンター [*bass-sentā*] bus station
バス停 [*bass-tei*] bus stop
バスターミナル [*bass-tāminaru*]
  bus terminal
乗車は前扉から [*jōsha wa mae-tobira kara*] enter at front door
降車は後扉から [*kōsha wa ushiro-tobira kara*] exit at rear door
料金箱 [*ryōkim-bako*] fare box
運賃箱 [*unchin-bako*] fare box
駅前 [*eki-mae*] in front of the station
市バス [*shi-bass*] municipal bus
都営バス [*to-ei-bass*] municipal bus
  (Tokyo)
回送 [*kaisō*] out of service
次は停車 [*tsugi wa teisha*] stopping
  at the next stop
運賃表 [*unchin-hyō*] table of fares

CINEMAS/MOVIE THEATERS

成人映画 [*seijin'eiga*] adult film
前売券 [*mae-uriken*]
  advance booking
満席 [*manseki*] all seats taken
マンガ映画 [*man-ga eiga*] cartoon
映画館 [*eigakan*] cinema,
  movie theater
入口 [*iriguchi*] entrance
出口 [*deguchi*] exit
映画 [*eiga*] film, movie
満員 [*man'in*] full
男子用 [*danshi-yō*] gentlemen,
  men's room
時代劇 [*jidai geki*] historical play/
  movie
女子用 [*joshi-yō*] ladies, ladies' room

未成年者入場無効 [*miseinensha-nyūjō mukō*] minors not admitted
未成年おことわり [*miseinen'okotowari*]
  minors not admitted
立入禁止 [*tachi-iri kinshi*] no entry
禁煙 [*kin'en*] no smoking
上映中 [*jōeichū*] now showing
開場時間 [*kaijō jikan*] opening time
ピンク映画 [*pinku eiga*]
  pornographic film
ポルノ [*poruno*] pornography
指定席 [*shtei seki*] reserved seat
座席 [*zaseki*] seat
ロードショー [*rōdoshō*]
  special release
お立見席 [*otachimi seki*]
  standing room only
字幕 [*jimak*] subtitles
切符 [*kip-p*] ticket
切符売り場 [*kip-pu uriba*]
  ticket office
御手洗 [*otearai*] toilets, rest rooms
洋画 [*yōga*] Western film (i.e. from
  the West, not cowboys)

CLOTHING LABELS

毛100% [*ke hyak pāsento*] 100% wool
アクリル [*akuriru*] acrylic
コットン [*kot-ton*] cotton
綿 [*men*] cotton
ドライクリーニング [*dorai kurīning-g*]
  dry clean
ドライ [*dorai*] dry clean
手洗い [*tearai*] hand-wash
取扱い方 [*toriatskai-kata*]
  instructions
低 [*tei*] low iron
日本製 [*Nihonsei*] made in Japan
中 [*chū*] medium iron
ナイロン [*nairon*] nylon
ポリエステル [*poriesteru*] polyester
レーヨン [*rēyon*] rayon

絹 [*kinu*] silk
シルク [*shiruk*] silk
サイズ [*saiz*] size

COUNTRIES AND NATIONALITIES

アメリカ [*Amerika*] America
米国 [*Beikok*] America
アメリカ人 [*Amerika-jin*] American
オーストラリア [*Ōstoraria*] Australia
カナダ [*Kanada*] Canada
中国 [*Chūgok*] China
イギリス [*Igiriss*] England, Britain
英国 [*Eikok*] Britain
英国人 [*Eikok-jin*] Briton
ヨーロッパ [*Yōrop-pa*] Europe
フランス [*Huranss*] France
ドイツ [*Doits*] Germany
独 [*Doku*] Germany
  (*in compounds*)
インド [*Indo*] India
日本 [*Nihon*] Japan
日本人 [*Nihon-jin*] Japanese
韓国 [*Kankok*] Korea
…人 [*…jin*] person
ロシア [*Roshia*] Russia
ソ連 [*Soren*] Russia, the USSR
スペイン [*Spein*] Spain
東洋 [*Tōyō*] The East
西洋 [*Seiyō*] The West
西洋人 [*Seiyō-jin*] Westerner

CUSTOMS

税関 [*zeikan*] customs
税関検査 [*zeikan-kensa*]
  customs check
出国 [*shuk-kok*] departure
入国カード [*nyūkoku-kādo*] entry card
入国 [*nyūkok*] entry into a country,
  immigration
外国人 [*gaikoku-jin*]
  foreign nationals

入国審査 [*nyūkoku-shinsa*]
  immigration control
日本人 [*Nihon-jin*]
  Japanese nationals
検疫 [*ken'eki*] quarantine

DAYS OF THE WEEK

月曜日 [*getsuyōbi*] Monday
火曜日 [*kayōbi*] Tuesday
水曜日 [*suiyōbi*] Wednesday
木曜日 [*mokuyōbi*] Thursday
金曜日 [*kin'yōbi*] Friday
土曜日 [*doyōbi*] Saturday
日曜日 [*nichiyōbi*] Sunday
一週間 [*ish-shūkan*] one week

DEPARTMENT STORE SECTIONS

オーディオ製品 [*ōdio seihin*]
  audio, hi-fi
バーゲン [*bāgen*] bargains
ケーキ [*kēki*] cakes
子供服（売場）[*kodomo-huk (uriba)*]
  children's wear
陶器 [*tōki*] china
化粧品 [*keshōhin*] cosmetics
電気製品 [*denki seihin*]
  electrical goods
食品 [*shokuhin*] food
家具 [*kagu*] furniture
庭園 [*teien*] garden centre/center
きもの/着物 [*kimono*] kimonos
台所用品 [*daidokoro yōhin*]
  kitchen goods
婦人服（売場）[*hujin-huk (uriba)*]
  ladies' wear
スタンド [*stando*] lamps
紳士服（売場）[*shinshi-huk (uriba)*]
  menswear
お中元 [*ochūgen*] mid-year gifts
香水 [*kōsui*] perfumery
食堂 [*shokudō*] restaurant

屋上 [*okujō*] roof

スポーツ用品 [*spōts yōhin*]
sports goods

文房具 [*bumbōgu*] stationery

おもちゃ（売場） [*omocha (uriba)*]
toys

下着売場 [*shtagi uriba*] underwear

歳末売出し [*saimatsu-uridashi*]
year-end sale

お歳暮 [*oseibo*] year-end gifts

DOCTORS *see* MEDICAL

DO NOT ...

動物にえさを与えないで下さい
[*dōbuts ni esa o ataenaide kudasai*]
do not feed the animals

お手をふれないで下さい [*ote o*
hurenaide kudasai] do not touch

さわるな [*sawaruna*] do not touch

…おことわり [*... okotowari*]
... forbidden

芝生に入らないで下さい [*shibahu ni*
hairanaide kudasai] keep off the
grass

入場おことわり [*nyūjō okotowari*]
no admittance

関係者以外の立入禁止 [*kankei-sha igai*
no tachi-iri-kinshi] no admittance
for unauthorized personnel

立入禁止 [*tachi-iri-kinshi*] no entry

禁漁区 [*kin-gyo-ku*] no fishing

左折禁止 [*sasets kinshi*] no left turn

駐車禁止 [*chūsha kinshi*] no parking

写真禁止 [*shashin kinshi*]
no photographs

右折禁止 [*usets kinshi*] no right turn

禁煙 [*kin'en*] no smoking

停車禁止 [*teisha kinshi*] no stopping

禁泳区 [*kin'ei-ku*] no swimming

通行止 [*tsūkō-dome*] no through
traffic

通行禁止 [*tsūkō-kinshi*] no through
traffic

DRINKS

アペリティフ [*aperitif*] aperitif

りんごジュース [*ringo jūss*]
apple juice

アップルジュース [*ap-puru jūss*]
apple juice

げんまいちゃ/玄米茶 [*gem-mai-cha*]
'ban-cha' tea with roasted rice

ビール [*bīru*] beer

ブラックコーヒー [*burak-ku kōhī*]
black coffee

紅茶 [*kōcha*] black tea

ブランデー [*burandē*] brandy

シャンペン [*shampen*] champagne

ばんちゃ/番茶 [*ban-cha*] cheap tea
with large leaves

ココア [*kokoa*] cocoa

コーヒー [*kōhī*] coffee

クリームコーヒー [*kurīm kōhī*]
coffee with whipped cream

コーヒー牛乳 [*kōhī gyūnyū*]
coffee-flavo(u)red milk

コニャック [*konyak-k*] cognac

コーラ [*kōra*] cola (*tm*)

しょうちゅう/焼酎 [*shōchū*]
distilled rice spirit

なまビール/生ビール [*nama bīru*]
draught/draft beer

からくち/辛口 [*karakuchi*] dry

オレンジファンタ [*orenji fanta*]
'fanta' orange (*tm*)

ジン [*jin*] gin

ジンレモン [*jin remon*] gin and
lemon

ジントニック [*jin tonik-k*] gin and
tonic

ジンフィズ [*jin fiz*] gin fizz

グレープジュース [*gurēp jūss*]
grape juice

グレープフルーツジュース [gurēp-hurūts jūss] grapefruit juice

ソーダ水 [sōda sui] green, sweet soda pop

アイスコーヒー [aiss kōhī] iced coffee

アイスティー [aiss tī] iced tea

おひや/お冷 [ohiya] iced water

お茶 [ocha] Japanese tea

こぶちゃ/昆布茶 [kobu-cha] kelp tea

レモンスカッシュ [remon skash] lemon squash

レモンティー [remon tī] lemon tea

レモネード [remonēdo] lemonade

サイダー [saidā] lemonade

ライムジュース [raim jūss] lime juice

リキュール [rikyūru] liqueur

マルティーニ [marutīni] martini

せんちゃ/煎茶 [sen-cha] medium-grade green tea

メロンジュース [meron jūss] melon juice

ミルク [miruk] milk

ぎゅうにゅう/牛乳 [gyūnyū] milk

ミルクセーキ [miruk sēki] milkshake

ミネラルウォーター [mineraru uōtā] mineral water

オレンジジュース [orenji jūss] orange juice

オレンジスカッシュ [orenji skash] orange squash

オレンジエード [orenjiēdo] orangeade

パインジュース [pain jūss] pineapple juice

ポートワイン [pōtowain] port

まっちゃ/抹茶 [mat-cha] powdered green tea

あかワイン/赤ワイン [aka wain] red wine

さけ/酒 [sake] rice wine, sake

にほんしゅ/日本酒 [nihonshu] rice wine

にほんしゅひや/日本酒冷 [nihonshu hiya] cold rice wine

にほんしゅあつかん/日本酒熱燗 [nihonshu atskan] hot rice wine

じざけ/地酒 [ji-zake] local rice wine

ますざけ/升酒 [masu-zake] rice wine served in wooden box cup

ロゼワイン [roze wain] rosé wine

ラム [ram] rum

シェリー [sherī] sherry

スパークリング [spākuring-g] sparkling

いちごジュース [ichigo jūss] strawberry juice

いちご牛乳 [ichigo gyūnyū] strawberry milk

ストロベリーミルク [storoberī miruk] strawberry milk

あまくち/甘口 [amakuchi] sweet

ほうじちゃ/焙茶 [hōji-cha] tea made with roasted 'ban-cha' leaves

ミルクティー [miruk tī] tea with milk

トマトジュース [tomato jūss] tomato juice

トニックウォーター [tonik-k uōtā] tonic

ベルモット [berumot-to] vermouth

ウォッカ [uok-ka] vodka

みず/水 [mizu] water

こおりみず/氷水 [kōri mizu] water with ice

ウイスキー [uiskī] whisky

ハイボール [haibōru] whisky and soda

オンザロック [onzarok-k] whisky on the rocks

みずわり [mizuwari] whisky with water

ミルクコーヒー [miruku kōhī] white coffee, coffee with milk

しろワイン/白ワイン [*shiro wain*]
white wine

ワイン [*wain*] wine

ぶどうしゅ/葡萄酒 [*budōshu*] wine

EATING AND DRINKING PLACES

けいしょくきっさ/軽食喫茶
[*keishoku-kiss-sa*]
coffee shop serving light meals

きっさてん/喫茶店 [*kiss-saten*]
coffee shop

かっぽう/割烹 [*kap-pō*] expensive,
quality restaurant

りょうてい/料亭 [*ryōtei*] expensive,
quality restaurant

のみや/飲み屋 [*nomiya*] local bar

レストラン [*restoran*] restaurant

りょうりや/料理屋 [*ryōriya*]
restaurant

しょくどう/食堂 [*shokudō*]
restaurant

こりょうりや/小料理屋 [*koryōriya*]
small local restaurant

めしや/飯屋 [*meshiya*] small local
restaurant

スナック [*snak-k*] snackbar

スナックバー [*snak-kbā*] snackbar

けいしょく/軽食 [*keishok*] snackbar

しょうじんりょうりや/精進料理屋
[*shōjin ryōriya*] vegetarian
restaurant

しょくじどころ/食事所
[*shokujidokoro*] very small local
restaurant

ELEVATORS *see* LIFTS

EMERGENCIES

救急車 [*kyūkyū-sha*] ambulance

非常呼び出し [*hijō-yobidashi*]
emergency call

非常口 [*hijō-guchi*] emergency exit

非常出口 [*hijō-deguchi*]
emergency exit

救急病院 [*kyūkyū-byōin*]
emergency hospital

救命袋 [*kyūmei-bukuro*]
emergency kit; fire escape chute

救助袋 [*kyūjo-bukuro*] emergency kit

非常電話 [*hijō-denwa*] emergency
telephone

火災報知器 [*kasai-hōchi-ki*] fire
alarm

消火器 [*shōka-ki*] fire extinguisher

消火栓 [*shōka-sen*] fire hydrant,
fireplug

応急手当 [*ōkyū-teate*] first aid

救急箱 [*kyūkyū-bako*] first aid box

救命ボート [*kyūmei-bōto*] lifeboat

110番 [*hyak-tōban*] police

警報ランプ [*keihō-ramp*]
warning light

FOOD

Starters

アスパラガス [*asparagass*] asparagus

キャビア [*kyabia*] caviar

セロリ [*serori*] celery

はまぐり/蛤 [*hamaguri*] clams

かに/蟹 [*kani*] crab

フルーツジュース [*hurūts jūss*]
fruit juice

ハム [*ham*] ham

にしん/鰊 [*nishin*] herring

おつまみ [*otsumami*]
Japanese-style appetizer

いせえび/伊勢海老 [*ise-ebi*] lobster

メロン [*meron*] melon

マッシュルーム [*mash-shurūm*]
mushrooms

かき [*kaki*] oysters

くるまえび/車海老 [*kuruma-ebi*]
prawns

さかなのたまご/魚の卵 [*sakana no
tamago*] roe

サラダ [*sarada*] salad
サラミ [*sarami*] salami
さけ/鮭 [*sake*] salmon
ソーセージ [*sōsēji*] sausage
こえび/小海老 [*ko-ebi*] shrimps
スープ [*sūp*] soup
まぐろ/鮪 [*maguro*] tuna fish
すいか/西瓜 [*suika*] watermelon

Soups

アスパラのスープ [*aspara no sūp*]
  asparagus soup
にんじんのポタージュ/
  人参のポタージュ [*ninjin no potāj*]
  carrot soup
とりのスープ/鳥のスープ [*tori no
  sūp*] chicken soup
チキンポタージュ [*chikim potāj*]
  chicken soup
すましじる/清汁 [*sumashijiru*]
  clear soup with vegetables or fish
すいもの/吸い物 [*suimono*]
  clear soup with vegetables or fish
きのこのスープ/茸のスープ [*kinoko
  no sūp*] clear soup with
  mushrooms
コンソメスープ [*konsome sūp*]
  consommé
やさいのクリームスープ/野菜の
  クリームスープ [*yasai no kurīm
  sūp*] cream of vegetable soup
マッシュルームのポタージュ [*mash-
  shurūm no potāj*] mushroom soup
オニオングラタンスープ [*onion
  guratan sūp*] onion soup au gratin
みそしる/味噌汁 [*misoshiru*]
  soup with 'miso' or bean paste
しるもの/汁物 [*shirumono*] soups
スープ [*sūp*] soups
ほうれんそうのポタージュ [*hōrensō no
  potāj*] spinach soup
トマトスープ [*tomato sūp*]
  tomato soup

Eggs and Egg Dishes

ベーコンエッグ [*bēkon'eg-g*]
  bacon and eggs
かにたま/蟹卵 [*kani-tama*]
  crab omelet(te)
ゆでたまご/茹卵 [*yude-tamago*]
  boiled egg(s)
たまご/卵 [*tamago*] egg(s)
たまご/玉子 [*tamago*] egg(s)
めだまやき/目玉焼き [*medama-yaki*]
  fried egg(s)
ハムエッグ [*hamu-eg-g*] ham and
  eggs
たまごやき/卵焼き [*tamago-yaki*]
  Japanese-style omelet(te)
オムレツ [*omurets*] omelet(te)
オムライス [*omuraiss*] omelet(te)
  with rice
パンケーキ [*pankēki*] pancake(s)
ポーチドエッグ [*pōchido-eg-g*]
  poached egg(s)
おやこどんぶり/親子丼 [*oyako-
  domburi*] rice topped with chicken
  and onion cooked in egg
たまごどんぶり/卵丼 [*tamago-
  domburi*] rice topped with onion
  cooked in egg
ちゃわんむし/茶碗蒸し [*chawam-
  mushi*] savo(u)ry custard with
  egg and fish
スコッチエッグ [*skotchi-eg-g*]
  Scotch egg, hard-boiled egg in
  sausage meat
はんじゅくたまご/半熟卵 [*hanjuku-
  tamago*] soft-boiled egg(s)
たまごとじ/卵綴 [*tamago-toji*]
  soft scrambled eggs with
  vegetables
たまごスープ/卵スープ [*tamago-sūp*]
  soup with egg
たまごどうふ/卵豆腐 [*tamago-dōhu*]
  steamed egg custard (savo(u)ry)

Fish and Fish Dishes

あわび/鮑　[*awabi*]　abalone,
　type of shellfish
赤貝　[*akagai*]　arkshell
ほっけ　[*hok-ke*]　Atka mackerel
いいだこ　[*i-dako*]　baby octopus
すずき　[*suzuki*]　bass
めばる　[*mebaru*]　black rockfish
ふぐ　[*hugu*]　blowfish
みる貝　[*mirugai*]　boiled round clams
かつお　[*katsuo*]　bonito, tunny
かば焼　[*kabayaki*]　broiled and
　basted eel
うな重　[*unajū*]　broiled eel on rice
こい　[*koi*]　carp
並　[*nami*]　cheaper selection
あじのたたき　[*aji no tataki*]
　chopped raw horse mackerel in a
　spicy sauce
はまぐり　[*hamaguri*]　clams
たら　[*tara*]　cod
たらこ　[*tarako*]　cod roe
あなご　[*anago*]　conger eel
しじみ　[*shijimi*]　corbicula
かに　[*kani*]　crab
うなぎ　[*unagi*]　eel
上　[*jō*]　expensive selection
うおすき/魚すき　[*uoski*]　fish dish
こち　[*kochi*]　flathead
ひらめ　[*hirame*]　flounder
とびうお　[*tobi-uo*]　flying fish
わかさぎ　[*wakasagi*]
　freshwater smelt
こはだ　[*kohada*]　gizzard shad
はぜ　[*haze*]　goby
きんめだい　[*kim-me-dai*]
　gold-eyed bream
うな丼　[*unadon*]　grilled eel on rice
たちうお　[*tachi-uo*]　hairtail
さより　[*sayori*]　hemiramph
にしん　[*nishin*]　herring
かずのこ　[*kazunoko*]　herring roe
あじ　[*aji*]　horse mackerel

くらげ　[*kurage*]　jellyfish
たらばがに　[*taraba-gani*]　king crab
伊勢えび　[*ise-ebi*]　lobster
さば　[*saba*]　mackerel
しゃこ　[*shako*]　mantis crab shrimp
ムール貝　[*mūrugai*]　mussels
たこ　[*tako*]　octopus
かき　[*kaki*]　oyster
さんま　[*sam-ma*]　Pacific saury
かます　[*kamass*]　pike
とろ　[*toro*]　pink belly of tuna fish
ちゅうとろ　[*chū-toro*]　pink tuna fish
車えび　[*kuruma-ebi*]　prawns
にじます　[*niji-mass*]　rainbow trout
さしみ　[*sashimi*]　raw fish
にぎりずし　[*nigiri-zushi*]
　raw fish on riceballs
すし　[*sushi*]　raw fish on riceballs
寿司　[*sushi*]　raw fish on riceballs
ふぐさし　[*hugu-sashi*]
　raw sliced blowfish
てっかどんぶり　[*tek-ka-domburi*]
　rice in a bowl topped with slices of
　raw tuna fish
いなだ　[*inada*]　round yellowtail
さけ　[*sake*]　salmon
いくら　[*ikura*]　salmon roe
いわし　[*iwashi*]　sardines
帆立て貝　[*hotategai*]　scallops
貝柱　[*kai-bashira*]　scallops' eyes
たい　[*tai*]　sea bream
はも　[*hamo*]　sea eel
なまこ　[*namako*]　sea slug
きす　[*kiss*]　sea smelt
ほや　[*hoya*]　sea squirt
うに　[*uni*]　sea urchin
うなぎ定食　[*unagi-teishok*]
　set meal with eel
あさり　[*asari*]　short-necked clams
ふぐちり　[*hugu-chiri*]　shredded
　blowfish in vegetable chowder
えび　[*ebi*]　shrimps
活魚　[*iki-uo*]　sliced raw fish

arranged as a whole fish

芝えび [*shiba ebi*] small shrimps

ししゃも [*shishamo*] smelt

スモークサーモン [*sumōk-sāmon*]
  smoked salmon

舌平目 [*shta-birame*] sole

しょうゆ [*shōyu*] soy sauce

さわら [*sawara*] Spanish mackerel

いか [*ika*] squid

あゆ [*ayu*] sweet smelt

かじき [*kajiki*] swordfish

あまだい [*amadai*] tilefish

さざえ [*sazae*] top-shell

ます [*mass*] trout

まぐろ [*maguro*] tuna fish

かれい [*karei*] turbot

鯨 [*kujira*] whale

しらす [*shirass*] whitebait

白魚 [*shira-uo*] whitefish

ぶり [*buri*] yellowtail

はまち [*hamachi*] young yellowtail

Meat and Meat Dishes

ベーコン [*bēkon*] bacon

バーベキュー [*bābekyū*] barbecue

ぎゅうにく/牛肉 [*gyūnik*] beef

ビーフ [*bīf*] beef

てっぱんやき/鉄板焼 [*tep-pan'yaki*]
  beef and vegetables grilled at the
  table

ぎゅうしょうがやき/牛生姜焼
  [*gyūshōgayaki*] beef cooked in soy
  sauce with ginger

ビフテキ [*bihuteki*] beef steak

ぎゅうてりやき/牛照焼 [*gyūteriyaki*]
  beef grilled with soy sauce

むねにく/胸肉 [*munenik*] breast

にわとり [*niwatori*] chicken

にわとりのむねにく [*niwatori no
  munenik*] chicken breast

あばらにく/肋肉 [*abaranik*] chops

コロッケ [*korok-ke*] croquettes

カツレツ [*katsrets*] cutlets

とんかつ/豚カツ [*tonkats*]
  deep-fried pork cutlets

カツどん/カツ丼 [*katsudon*]
  deep-fried pork on rice

ヒレにく/ヒレ肉 [*hirenik*] fillet

やきにく/焼肉 [*yakinik*] fried pork
  marinated in soy sauce

がちょう [*gachō*] goose

くしやき/串焼き [*kushiyaki*]
  grilled meat on skewers

ハム [*ham*] ham

ハンバーグ [*hambāg*] hamburger

じんぞう・腎臓 [*jinzō*] kidney

こひつじのにく・子羊の肉 [*kohitsuji
  no nik*] lamb

こひつじ・子羊 [*ko-hitsuji*] lamb

ラム [*ram*] lamb

ラムにく/ラム肉 [*ramnik*] lamb

レバー [*rebā*] liver

にく/肉 [*nik*] meat

にくだんご/肉団子 [*nikudan-go*]
  meatballs

ひきにく/挽肉 [*hikinik*]
  minced meat, ground beef

ロールキャベツ [*rōrukyabets*]
  minced meat/ground beef in
  rolled cabbage

マトン [*maton*] mutton

ひつじのにく/羊の肉 [*hitsuji no nik*]
  mutton

ほねつき/骨付き [*honetski*]
  on the bone

きじ [*kiji*] pheasant

ぶたにく/豚肉 [*butanik*] pork

ポーク [*pōk*] pork

ほねつきぶたにく/骨付き豚肉
  [*honetski butanik*] pork chop

ぶたしょうがやき/豚生姜焼
  [*butashōgayaki*] pork cooked in soy
  sauce with ginger

カツカレー [*katskarē*]
  pork cutlets with curry

ぶたてりやき/豚照焼 [*butateriyaki*]

pork grilled with soy sauce

とりりょうり/鳥料理 [*tori-ryōri*]
  poultry dishes

うずら [*uzura*] quail

カレーライス [*karēraiss*]
  rice with curry-flavo(u)red stew

ローストビーフ [*rōstobīf*] roast beef

ローストチキン [*rōstochikin*]
  roast chicken

ローストポーク [*rōstopōk*] roast pork

ソーセージ [*sōsēji*] sausage

サーロイン [*sāroin*] sirloin

やきとり/焼き鳥 [*yakitori*]
  skewered fowl cooked over a grill

ラムのくしやき/ラムの串焼き
  [*ram-no-kushiyaki*] skewered lamb

バターやき/バター焼 [*batāyaki*]
  sliced beef or pork fried in butter

しゃぶしゃぶ [*shabu-shabu*]
  sliced beef with vegetables boiled
  at the table

すきやき/すき焼/すき焼き [*skiyaki*]
  'sukiyaki', sliced beef with
  vegetables in sweet soy sauce
  cooked at the table

スペアリブ [*speyarib*] spare ribs

すずめ [*suzume*] sparrow

ステーキ [*stēki*] steak

シチューにく/シチュー肉 [*shchūnik*]
  stewing meat

タン [*tan*] tongue

した/舌 [*shta*] tongue

もつ [*mots*] tripe

しちめんちょう/七面鳥
  [*shchimenchō*] turkey

こうしのにく/子牛の肉
  [*ko-ushi no nik*] veal

Rice and Rice Dishes

うなじゅう [*unajū*] boiled eel on rice

…どんぶり/…丼 [*… domburi*]
  'domburi', bowl of rice with
  something on top

うなぎどんぶり [*unagi domburi*]
  'domburi' with broiled eel

てんどん/天丼 [*tendon*]
  'domburi' with deep-fried
  shrimps

たまごどんぶり/卵丼 [*tamago
  domburi*] 'domburi' with onions
  cooked in egg

ちゅうかどんぶり/中華丼 [*chūka
  domburi*] 'domburi' with pork
  and vegetables

にくどん/肉丼 [*nikudon*]
  'domburi' with sliced beef

カツどん/カツ丼 [*katsudon*]
  'domburi' with deep-fried
  breaded pork cutlet

おやこどんぶり/親子丼 [*oyako
  domburi*] 'domburi' with
  chicken and egg

チャーハン [*chāhan*] fried rice

オムライス [*omuraiss*] plain
  omelet(te) wrapped around rice

ごはん/御飯 [*gohan*] rice

ライス [*raiss*] rice

ぞうすい [*zōsui*] rice boiled in
  seasoned soup

もち/餅 [*mochi*] rice cakes

おちゃづけ/お茶漬 [*ochazuke*]
  rice in tea or fish broth

かまめし/釜飯 [*kamameshi*]
  rice steamed in fish bouillon with
  pieces of meat, fish and vegetable

チキンライス [*chikin raiss*]
  rice with chicken

カレーライス [*karēraiss*]
  rice with curry-flavo(u)red stew

おにぎり [*onigiri*] riceballs

ハヤシライス [*hayashi raiss*] sliced or
  hashed beef with rice

Vegetables

こんにゃく [*kon-nyak*]
  arum root gelatin

アスパラガス [*asparagass*] asparagus

アスパラ [*aspara*] asparagus

なす [*nass*] aubergine, eggplant

プチトマト [*puchi-tomato*]
baby tomatoes

竹の子 [*takenoko*] bamboo shoots

とうふ [*tōhu*] bean curd

もやし [*moyashi*] bean sprouts

豆 [*mame*] beans

枝豆 [*eda-mame*]
boiled green soybeans

山菜煮つけ [*sansai-nitske*]
boiled mountain greens with
seasoning

おひたし [*ohitashi*]
boiled spinach with seasoning

そら豆 [*sora-mame*] broad beans

ブロッコリー [*burok-korī*] broccoli

でんがく [*den-gak*]
broiled beancurd on a stick

しめじ [*shimeji*]
brown button mushrooms

芽キャベツ [*mekyabets*]
Brussels sprouts

ごぼう [*gobō*] burdock root

キャベツ [*kyabets*] cabbage

にんじん [*ninjin*] carrots

カリフラワー [*karihurawā*]
cauliflower

セロリ [*serori*] celery

白菜 [*hak-sai*] Chinese cabbage

しいたけ [*shītake*] Chinese
mushrooms

菊の花 [*kiku-no-hana*]
chrysanthemum petals

春菊 [*shun-gik*]
chrysanthemum greens

とうもろこし [*tōmorokoshi*] corn

きゅうり [*kyūri*] cucumber

かんぴょう [*kampyō*]
dried gourd shavings

なめこ [*nameko*] edible fungus

きくらげ [*kikurage*]
edible tree fungus

きくじしゃ [*kikujisha*] endives

みそ [*miso*]
fermented soybean paste

なっとう [*nat-tō*]
fermented soybeans

油揚げ [*abura-age*] fried bean curd

きんぴら [*kimpira*]
fried burdock root and carrot

しょうが [*shōga*] ginger

さやいんげん [*saya-ingen*]
green beans

ピーマン [*pīman*] green pepper

ししとう [*shishtō*]
green pepper (small)

三つ葉 [*mitsuba*] Japanese celery

みょうが [*myōga*] Japanese ginger

わさび [*wasabi*]
Japanese horseradish

まつたけ [*matstake*]
Japanese mushrooms

せり [*seri*] Japanese parsley

さんしょう [*sanshō*]
Japanese pepper

この芽 [*konome*]
Japanese pepper leaves

きくいも [*kiku-imo*]
Jerusalem artichoke

いんげん豆 [*ingem-mame*]
kidney beans

たかな [*takana*] leaf mustard

小松菜 [*komatsna*] leafy cabbage

ねぎ [*negi*] leek

しそ [*shiso*] lemon-mint leaf

レタス [*retass*] lettuce

れんこん [*renkon*] lotus root

さやえんどう [*saya-endō*]
mange tout

野菜盛合せ [*yasai-mori-awase*]
mixed vegetables

マッシュルーム [*mash-shurūm*]
mushrooms

きのこ [*kinoko*]

mushrooms (*general term*)

からし菜 [*karashina*] mustard greens

オクラ [*okura*] okra

玉ねぎ [*tamanegi*] onions

パセリ [*paseri*] parsley

えんどう豆 [*endō-mame*] peas

うめぼし [*umeboshi*] pickled plums

山いも [*yama-imo*] potato (type of)

ポテトサラダ [*poteto-sarada*]
potato salad

じゃがいも [*jagaimo*] potatoes

ポテト [*poteto*] potatoes

かぼちゃ [*kabocha*] pumpkin

はつか大根 [*hatska daikon*] radishes

菜の花 [*na-no-hana*] rape blossom

あずき [*adzuki*] red beans

しなちく [*shina-chik*]
salted Chinese bamboo

らっきょう [*rak-kyō*] scallion

にら [*nira*] scallion leek

わかめ [*wakame*] seaweed

昆布 [*kombu*] seaweed (thick)

のり [*nori*] seaweed (paper-like)

ひじき [*hijiki*] seaweed

ごま [*goma*] sesame seeds

大豆 [*daizu*] soybeans

ほうれん草 [*hōrensō*] spinach

しらたき [*shirataki*]
starch paste noodles

さつまいも [*satsuma-imo*]
sweet potatoes

コーン [*kōn*] sweetcorn

里芋 [*sato-imo*] taro

トマト [*tomato*] tomatoes

かぶ [*kabu*] turnips

野菜 [*yasai*] vegetables

クレソン [*kureson*] watercress

わけぎ [*wakegi*] Welsh onions

ふき [*huki*] wild butterbur

えのきだけ [*enokidake*]
yellow button mushrooms

たくあん [*takuan*]
yellow radish pickles

Salads

サラダ [*sarada*] salad

サラダ菜 [*sarada-na*] lettuce

生野菜 [*nama yasai*] fresh salad

ミックスサラダ [*mik-ks-sarada*]
mixed salad

ドレッシング [*doreshing-g*]
salad dressing

Noodles

うどんすき [*udon-ski*]
chicken and noodles boiled in
sweetened soy sauce

ラーメン/拉麺 [*rāmen*]
Chinese noodles

チャーシューメン [*chāshūmen*]
Chinese noodles in pork bouillon

みそラーメン/味噌ラーメン
[*miso-rāmen*] Chinese noodles dish
similar to 'chāshūmen' with
bean paste

チャンポン [*champon*]
Chinese noodles in salted bouillon
with vegetables

ひやむぎ/冷や麦 [*hiya mugi*]
like 'sōmen' but served cold

そば/蕎麦 [*soba*] buckwheat noodles

うどん [*udon*] thick, white,
wheatflour noodles

そうめん/素麺 [*sōmen*] thin, white,
wheatflour noodles

やきそば/焼そば [*yaki soba*]
noodles fried with small pieces of
vegetable

とろろそば/薯蕷蕎麦 [*tororo soba*]
noodles in fish bouillon topped
with paste made from a root

てんぷらそば/天麩羅蕎麦 [*tempura
soba*] noodles in fish bouillon
with deep-fried shrimps

おかめそば/お亀そば [*okame soba*]
noodles in fish bouillon with fish
dumplings

つきみそば/月見蕎麦 [tskimi soba]
noodles in fish bouillon with an
egg on top

にくなんばん/肉南蛮 [niku namban]
noodles in fish bouillon with pork
or beef

なめこうどん [nameko udon]
noodles in fish bouillon with small
mushrooms

たぬきうどん [tanuki udon]
noodles in fish bouillon with small
pieces of deep-fried flour

つきみうどん/月見うどん [tskimi
udon] noodles in fish bouillon,
with egg and fish paste

かけそば/掛蕎麦 [kake soba]
noodles in fish broth

きつねうどん [kitsune udon] noodles
in fish broth with bean curd

なべやきうどん/鍋焼きうどん
[nabe yaki udon] noodles in fish
broth with mushrooms, fish
paste and deep-fried shrimps

ザーサイそば [zāsai soba] noodles in
pork bouillon flavo(u)red with
Chinese pickles

もやしそば/萌そば [moyashi soba]
noodles in pork broth with bean
sprouts

あんかけそば/餡掛けそば [ankake
soba] noodles in thick bouillon
with fish paste and vegetables

ひやしちゅうか/冷し中華 [hiyashi
chūka] noodles served cold with
slices of meat and vegetable

ざるそば/笊蕎麦 [zaru soba]
noodles served cold, to be dipped
in soy sauce

もりそば/盛り蕎麦 [mori soba]
noodles served cold, to be dipped
in sweetened soy sauce

てんざる/天笊 [ten zaru]
'soba' served with deep-fried
shrimps

ギョーザそば/餃子そば [gyōza soba]
'soba' in broth with envelopes of
minced/ground meat

ごもくそば/五目そば [gomok soba]
'soba' in broth with pieces of
vegetable and meat

みそにこみうどん/味噌煮込み饂飩
[miso nikomi udon] thick noodles
and pork in fish broth
flavo(u)red with bean paste

カレーなんばん/カレー南蛮
[karē namban] 'udon' in curry-
flavo(u)red soup with pork or
beef

かもなんばん/鴨南蛮 [kamo namban]
'udon' in fish bouillon with
chicken or duck

Fruit and Nuts

アーモンド [āmondo] almonds

りんご/林檎 [rin-go] apples

バナナ [banana] bananas

さくらんぼ/桜ん坊 [sakurambo]
cherries

くり/栗 [kuri] chestnuts

ココナッツ [kokonats] coconut

いちじく/無花果 [ichijik] figs

くだもの/果物 [kudamono] fruit

フルーツ [hurūts] fruit

ぎんなん/銀杏 [gin-nan]
gingko nuts

グレープフルーツ [grēp-hurūts]
grapefruit

ぶどう/葡萄 [budō] grapes

ヘーゼルナッツ [hēzeru-nats]
hazelnuts

レモン [remon] lemon

メロン [meron] melon

オレンジ [orenji] oranges

もも/桃 [momo] peach

すいみつ/水蜜 [sui-mits]
(kind of white) peach

ピーナッツ [*pīnats*] peanuts
なし/梨 [*nashi*] pears
かき/柿 [*kaki*] persimmons
パイナップル [*painap-puru*]
pineapple
すもも/李 [*sumomo*] plums
ざくろ/石榴 [*zakuro*] pomegranate
いちご/苺 [*ichigo*] strawberries
みかん/蜜柑 [*mikan*] tangerines
くるみ/胡桃 [*kurumi*] walnuts
すいか/西瓜 [*suika*] watermelon

Desserts

アップルパイ [*ap-puru pai*]
apple pie
くずもち/葛餅 [*kuzu mochi*]
arrowroot triangles in brown
sugar syrup
うじきんとき/宇治金時 [*uji kintoki*]
crushed ice with green tea syrup
and a layer of sweet bean paste
さくらもち/桜餅 [*sakura mochi*]
bean jam rice cake wrapped in
cherry leaf
クッキー [*kuk-kī*] biscuits, cookies
ビスケット [*bisket-to*]
biscuits, cookies
ケーキ [*kēki*] cake
チーズケーキ [*chīz-kēki*] cheesecake
さくらんぼヨーグルト [*sakurambo
yōguruto*] cherry yoghurt
チョコレート [*chokorēto*] chocolate
チョコレートケーキ [*chokorēto kēki*]
chocolate cake
チョコレートアイスクリーム
[*chokorēto aiskurīm*] chocolate
ice cream
チョコレートムース [*chokorēto mūss*]
chocolate mousse
チョコレートプディング [*chokorēto
puding-g*] chocolate pudding
チョコレートサンデー [*chokorēto
sandē*] chocolate sundae

コーヒーゼリー [*kōhī zerī*]
coffee-flavo(u)red jelly
カスタードプリン [*kastādo purin*]
cream caramel
プリン [*purin*] cream caramel
シュークリーム [*shūkurīm*]
cream puff
クレープ [*kurēp*] crêpe
氷あずき [*kōri adzuki*] crushed ice on
sweet bean paste
うじごおり/宇治氷 [*uji gōri*]
crushed ice with green tea syrup
氷レモン [*kōri remon*]
crushed ice with lemon syrup
氷メロン [*kōri meron*]
crushed ice with melon syrup
氷いちご [*kōri ichigo*]
crushed ice with strawberry syrup
氷ミルク [*kōri miruk*]
crushed ice with sweetened milk
カスタード [*kastādo*] custard
デザート [*dezāto*] dessert
ドーナッツ [*dōnats*] doughnut
エクレア [*ekurea*] éclair
フルーツケーキ [*hurūts kēki*]
fruit cake
フルーツサラダ [*hurūts sarada*]
fruit cocktail
フルーツゼリー [*hurūts zerī*]
fruit jelly
みつまめ/蜜豆 [*mitsumame*]
gelatin cubes and sweet beans
with pieces of fruit
クリームみつまめ [*kurīm mitsumame*]
gelatin cubes mixed with sweet
bean, served with vanilla ice
cream and fruit
あんみつ/餡蜜 [*am-mits*]
gelatin cubes with sweet bean and
pieces of fruit
おはぎ/お萩 [*ohagi*]
glutinous rice and bean jam
いそまき/磯巻き [*iso-maki*] grilled

rice cake wrapped in seaweed

アイスクリーム [*aiskurīm*] ice cream

わがし/和菓子 [*wagashi*]
Japanese-style confection

ゼリー [*zerī*] jelly

レモンパイ [*remon pai*] lemon pie

レモンスフレ [*remon suhure*]
lemon soufflé

ムース [*mūss*] mousse

オレンジヨーグルト [*orenji yōguruto*]
orange yoghurt

ピーチメルバ [*pīchi meruba*]
peach melba

フルーツみつまめ [*hurūts mitsumame*]
pieces of fruit served with gelatin
cubes

パイナップル [*painap-puru*]
pineapple

パインヨーグルト [*pain yōguruto*]
pineapple yoghurt

おもち/お餅 [*omochi*] rice cakes

あべかわもち/安倍川餅
[*abekawa mochi*] rice cakes
covered in bean powder

おせんべい/お煎餅 [*osembei*]
rice crackers

しおせんべい/塩煎餅 [*shio-sembei*]
rice crackers flavo(u)red with soy
sauce

まんじゅう/饅頭 [*manjū*] rice-flour
cakes with bean jam

シャーベット [*shābet-to*] sherbet

ショートケーキ [*shōto kēki*]
shortcake

かきもち/かき餅 [*kaki mochi*]
small crackers with soy sauce
flavo(u)ring

ようかん/羊かん [*yōkan*]
soft, sweet bean paste

スフレ [*suhure*] soufflé

カステラ [*kastera*] sponge cake

いちご/苺 [*ichigo*] strawberries

ストロベリーアイスクリーム

[*storoberī aiskurīm*] strawberry
ice cream

ストロベリーサンデー [*storoberī
sandē*] strawberry sundae

いちごヨーグルト [*ichigo yōguruto*]
strawberry yoghurt

ところてん/心太 [*tokoroten*] strips
of gelatin in tangy soy sauce

おしるこ/お汁粉 [*oshiruko*]
sweet bean soup with rice cake

ぜんざい/善哉 [*zenzai*] thick
bean soup with rice cakes

バニラアイスクリーム [*banira
aiskurīm*] vanilla ice cream

クリームあんみつ [*kurīmu am-mits*]
vanilla ice cream on gelatin
cubes with sweet bean and fruit

もなか/最中 [*monaka*] wafers filled
with bean jam

洋菓子 [*yōgashi*]
Western-style confection

ヨーグルト [*yōguruto*] yoghurt

ヨーグルトムース [*yōguruto mūss*]
yoghurt mousse

Japanese Set Meals

定食 [*teishok*] set meal with rice,
soup, pickles and main dish

ひがわりていしょく/日変り定食
[*higawari teishok*]
'teishok' of the day

てんぷらていしょく/天麩羅定食
[*tempura teishok*] 'teishok' with
deep-fried seafood and
vegetables as the main dish

やきざかなていしょく/焼魚定食
[*yakizakana teishok*] 'teishok' with
grilled fish as the main dish

やきにくていしょく/焼肉定食
[*yakiniku teishok*] 'teishok' with
grilled meat as the main dish

とんかつていしょく/豚カツ定食
[*tonkats teishok*] 'teishok' with

pork as the main dish

さしみていしょく/刺身定食
[*sashimi teishok*] 'teishok' with
raw fish as the main dish

おひるのていしょく/御昼の定食
[*ohiru no teishok*] lunchtime
'teishok'

Lunch Boxes

弁当 [*bentō*] box lunch

チキン弁当 [*chikim bentō*]
'bentō' with pieces of fried
chicken

まくのうちべんとう/幕の内弁当
[*makuno-uchi bentō*] 'bentō',
with rice, meat and vegetables
(*the commonest variety*)

サンドイッチ弁当 [*sandoit-chi bentō*]
'bentō' of sandwiches

Sushi Dishes

すし [*sushi*] 'sushi',
raw fish on riceballs

あがり [*agari*] green tea at end of
'sushi' meal

さんまずし [*sam-ma-zushi*]
Kansai-style 'sushi' with Pacific
saury

五目寿司 [*gomoku-zushi*]
mixed 'sushi'

ちらし寿司 [*chirashi-zushi*]
mixed 'sushi' on rice, with
chopped vegetables, strips of
fried egg etc.

ばってら [*bat-tera*]
Osaka-style mackerel 'sushi'

がり [*gari*] pickled slices of ginger

かっぱまき [*kap-pa-maki*]
seasoned rice and cucumber
wrapped in seaweed

てっかまき/鉄火巻き [*tek-ka-maki*]
seasoned rice and tuna wrapped
in seaweed

おしんこまき [*oshinko-maki*]
seasoned rice rolled in seaweed

いなりずし [*inari-zushi*]
seasoned rice wrapped in fried
tofu (bean curd)

のり [*nori*] seaweed

のりまき [*nori-maki*] sliced roll of
rice, vegetables and fish powder,
wrapped in seaweed

むらさき [*murasaki*]
soy sauce for 'sushi'

わさび [*wasabi*] very sharp
horseradish served with 'sushi'

Snacks

ビスケット [*bisket-to*]
biscuits, cookies

パン [*pan*] bread

ロールパン [*rōrupan*] bread roll

ケーキ [*kēki*] cake

チーズロール [*chīzurōru*] cheese roll

チーズサンドイッチ [*chīz sandoit-chi*]
cheese sandwich

チーズバーグ [*chīzbāg*]
cheeseburger

ポテトフライ [*poteto hurai*]
chips, French fries

チョコレート [*chokorēto*] chocolate

おかし/御菓子 [*okashi*]
confectionery

ポテトチップ [*poteto chip-p*]
crisps, potato chips

ハムサンド [*hamusando*]
ham sandwich

ハンバーグ [*hambāg*] hamburger

ホットドッグ [*hot-to dog-g*] hotdog

アイスクリーム [*aiskurīm*] ice cream

サラダ [*sarada*] salad

サンドイッチ [*sandoit-chi*] sandwich

スパゲッティ [*spageti*] spaghetti

トースト [*tōsto*] toast

ツナサンド [*tsunasando*]
tuna sandwich

Chinese Food

マーボーどうふ/マーボー豆腐
[*mābō-dōhu*] bean-curd in spicy
soup mixture

中華まんじゅう/中華饅頭
[*chūka manjū*] Chinese dumplings
(with meat or sweet beans)

ちゅうかりょうり/中華料理
[*chūka ryōri*] Chinese food

ラーメン/拉麺 [*rāmen*]
Chinese noodles (usually in pork
broth)

かにたま/蟹卵 [*kanitama*]
crab omelet(te)

にくからあげ/肉唐揚 [*niku kara-age*]
deep-fried pieces of pork or
chicken

ギョーザ/餃子 [*gyōza*]
dumplings stuffed with minced/
ground pork

ワンタンメン/饂飩麺 [*wantam-men*]
flour dumplings with pork in
bouillon with noodles

ヤキソバ/焼き蕎麦 [*yakisoba*]
fried noodles

はっぽうさい/八宝菜 [*hap-pō sai*]
fried pork with vegetables

チャーハン/焼飯 [*chāhan*] fried rice

やさいいため/野菜炒め [*yasai itame*]
fried vegetables

にくだんご/肉団子 [*niku dango*]
meatballs

にくみそそば/肉味噌蕎麦
[*niku miso soba*] noodles with spicy
'miso' meat sauce (*fermented
soybean paste*)

チャーシューメン [*chāshūmen*]
noodles in bouillon with slices of
pork

みそラーメン/味噌拉麺 [*miso rāmen*]
noodles in pork broth with
'miso' (*fermented soybean
paste*)

もやしそば/萌蕎麦 [*moyashi soba*]
noodles in pork broth with
beansprouts

タンメン/湯麺 [*tam-men*] noodles in
pork broth with vegetables

チャンポン [*champon*]
noodles in salted bouillon with
pork and vegetables

やさいスープ/野菜スープ [*yasai sūp*]
pork-flavo(u)red vegetable soup

ちゅうかどんぶり/中華丼
[*chūka domburi*]
rice covered in a thick sauce
with pork and vegetables

シューマイ/焼売 [*shūmai*]
small steamed balls of pork in thin
Chinese pastry

はるまき/春巻 [*harumaki*]
spring roll

すぶた/酢豚 [*subuta*]
sweet and sour pork

Basics

トンカツソース [*tonkats sōss*]
brown sauce, mixture of tomato
ketchup and Worcester sauce

バター [*batā*] butter

味の素 [*aji-no-moto*]
flavo(u)r enhancer

にんにく [*nin-nik*] garlic

ジャム [*jam*] jam

ケチャップ [*kechap-p*] ketchup

マーマレード [*māmarēdo*]
marmalade

マヨネーズ [*mayonēz*] mayonnaise

からし/辛子 [*karashi*] mustard

あぶら/油 [*abura*] oil

こしょう/胡椒 [*koshō*] pepper

しお/塩 [*shio*] salt

ちょうみりょう/調味料 [*chōmiryō*]
seasoning

しょうゆ/醤油 [*shōyu*] soy sauce

さとう/砂糖 [*satō*] sugar

す/酢 [*su*] vinegar
ウスターソース [*ustā sōss*]
  Worcester sauce

Methods of Preparation
てんぴやきした/天火焼した
  [*tempiyaki shta*] baked
バーベキューした [*bābekyū shta*]
  barbecued
にた/煮た [*nita*] boiled
とろびでにた/とろ火で煮た
  [*torobi de nita*] braised
どなべでにた/土鍋で煮た
  [*donabe de nita*] casseroled
ほした/干した [*hoshta*] dried
あげた/揚げた [*ageta*] fried
やいた/焼いた [*yaita*] grilled
ミディアム [*midiam*] medium
つけた/漬けた [*tsketa*] pickled
なべやきした/鍋焼きした
  [*nabeyaki shta*] pot-roast
レア [*reya*] rare
ローストした [*rōsto shta*] roast
むした/蒸した [*mushta*] steamed
シチューした [*shchū shta*] stewed
つめものをした/詰物をした
  [*tsumemono o shta*] stuffed
なまやき/生焼き [*namayaki*]
  underdone
ウエルダン [*weru-dan*] well-done

Culinary Categories
やきとり/焼き鳥 [*yakitori*]
  barbecued chicken on skewers
ふぐりょうり/河豚料理 [*hugu ryōri*]
  blowfish cuisine
そば/蕎麦 [*soba*]
  buckwheat noodles
ろばたやき/炉端焼 [*robata-yaki*]
  charcoal-grilled fish and
  vegetables
ちゅうかりょうり/中華料理
  [*Chūka ryōri*] Chinese-style cuisine

かっぽう/割烹 [*kap-pō*]
  customer-requested Japanese-
  style cordon bleu dishes
てんぷら/天麩羅 [*tempura*]
  deep-fried seafood and vegetables
フランスりょうり/フラソス料理
  [*Huranss ryōri*] French-style
  cuisine
おでん/お田 [*oden*]
  hotchpotch of fish and vegetables
  boiled in fish broth
イタリアりょうり/イタリア料理
  [*Itaria ryōri*] Italian-style cuisine
すいもの/吸い物 [*suimono*]
  Japanese broth
かいせきりょうり/懐石料理
  [*kaiseki ryōri*] Japanese
  haute cuisine
よせなべ/寄せ鍋 [*yosenabe*]
  Japanese-style chowder
にほんりょうり/日本料理
  [*Nihon ryōri*] Japanese-style
  cuisine
おこのみやき/お好み焼
  [*okonomi-yaki*] Japanese-style
  pancake with many ingredients
なべもの/鍋物 [*nabemono*]
  meat, fish and vegetables cooked
  in a pot at the table
うどん/饂飩 [*udon*]
  noodles of a thick white
  wheatflour variety
さしみ/刺し身 [*sashimi*] raw fish
すし/寿司 [*sushi*]
  raw fish on rice balls
すし/鮨 [*sushi*]
  raw fish on rice balls
きょうどりょうり/郷土料理
  [*kyōdo ryōri*] regional specialities
かまめし/釜飯 [*kamameshi*]
  rice casserole dishes
しゃぶしゃぶ [*shabu-shabu*]
  sliced beef with vegetables boiled

at the table

おせちりょうり/御節料理
　[*osechi ryōri*] special dishes
　prepared at New Year

てっぱんやき/鉄板焼　[*tep-pan' yaki*]
　steak grilled on tableside griddle

しょうじんりょうり/精進料理
　[*shōjin ryōri*] vegetarian cuisine

そうめん/素麵　[*sōmen*] vermicelli of
　a very thin wheatflour variety
　served in ice-cold water

せいようりょうり/西洋料理
　[*seiyō ryōri*] Western-style cuisine

FOOD LABELS

開封後はなるべく早くお召しあがり
　ください　[*kaihūgo wa narubek
　hayaku omeshi-agari kudasai*]
　consume as soon as possible
　after opening

製造年月日　[*seizō nen-gap-pi*]
　date of manufacture

62.02.05製造　[*62.02.05 seizō*]
　date of manufacture:
　5.2.87 (UK)/2.5.87 (USA)

開封後は冷蔵庫などに入れて保存して
　下さい　[*kaihūgo wa reizōko nado ni
　irete hozon shte kudasai*]
　refrigerate after opening

保存料は使用しておりません
　[*hozonryō wa shiyō shte ori-masen*]
　no preservatives added

保存方法　[*hozon hōhō*]
　storage instructions

FORMS

住所　[*jūsho*] address

滞在住所　[*taizai jūsho*]
　address during stay

年令　[*nenrei*] age

外国人登録証明書
　[*gaikoku-jin tōrok shōmeisho*]

alien registration card

連絡先　[*renrak-saki*] contact address

税関申告用紙　[*zeikan-shinkok-yōshi*]
　customs declaration form

税関告知書　[*zeikan kok-chi sho*]
　customs declaration form

生年月日　[*seinen-gap-pi*]
　date of birth

用紙　[*yōshi*] form

氏名　[*shimei*] full name

身分証明書　[*mibun shōmei-sho*]
　ID card

出発予定日　[*shup-pats yotei hi*]
　intended date of departure

滞在日数　[*taizai niss-sū*]
　length of stay

泊数　[*haksū*] number of nights

お名前　[*onamae*] name

国籍　[*kokseki*] nationality

職業　[*shokugyō*] occupation

旅券番号　[*ryoken ban-gō*]
　passport number

パスポート番号　[*paspōto ban-gō*]
　passport number

訪日目的　[*hōnichi mokteki*]
　purpose of visit

アンケート　[*ankēto*] questionnaire

ご署名　[*goshomei*] signature

サイン　[*sain*] signature

ボールペンで御記入下さい　[*bōrupen
　de okinyū kudasai*] write in ink

GARAGES

自動車整備工場　[*jidōsha seibi kōjō*]
　auto repairs

故障　[*koshō*] breakdown

洗車　[*sensha*] car wash

ディーゼル油　[*dīzeruyu*] diesel oil

入口　[*iriguchi*] entrance

出口　[*deguchi*] exit

無料点検　[*muryō tenken*]
　free inspection

満タン　[*mantan*] full tank

ハイオク [*hai-ok*] high octane
軽油 [*keiyu*] light fuel for mopeds
オイル [*oiru*] oil
…実施中 [*... jish-shi-chū*] ... on offer
灯油 [*tōyu*] paraffin, kerosene
石油 [*sekiyu*] petrol, gas
ガソリン [*gasorin*] petrol, gas
ガソリンスタンド [*gasorin stando*]
　petrol/gas station
レギュラー [*regyurā*] regular, 2-star
点検サービス [*tenken sābiss*] service
スーパー [*sūpā*] super, premium
タイヤチェック [*taiya chek-k*]
　tyre/tire check
水 [*mizu*] water

GEOGRAPHICAL

岬 [*misaki*] cape, promontory
国 [*kuni*] country
東 [*higashi*] east
森 [*mori*] forest
温泉 [*onsen*] hot spring
島 [*shima*] island
湖 [*mizūmi*] lake
地図 [*chizu*] map
山 [*yama*] mountain
山脈 [*sam-myak*] mountain range
北 [*kita*] north
半島 [*hantō*] peninsula
県 [*ken*] prefecture
地方 [*chihō*] region, area
川 [*kawa*] river
河 [*kawa*] river
海 [*umi*] sea
南 [*minami*] south
頂上 [*chōjō*] summit
…市 [*shi*] town, city
谷 [*tani*] valley
村 [*mura*] village
火山 [*kazan*] volcano
滝 [*taki*] waterfall
西 [*nishi*] west

HAIRDRESSERS

理髪店 [*rihats-ten*] barber shop
床屋 [*tokoya*] barber shop
美容院 [*biyōin*] beauty parlo(u)r
ビューティサロン [*byūti-saron*]
　beauty salon
脱色 [*dash-shok*] bleach
ブロードライ [*burōdorai*] blow dry
色 [*iro*] colo(u)r
カット [*kat-to*] cut
調髪 [*chōhats*] hair cutting
ヘアスタイル [*heastairu*] hair style
洗髪 [*sempats*] hair washing
マニキュア [*manikyua*] manicure
マッサージ [*mass-sāji*] massage
パーマ [*pāma*] perm
ヘアセット [*hea-set-to*] set
シャンプーとセット [*shampū to set-to*]
　shampoo and set

HOSPITALS *see* MEDICAL

HOTELS

冷房 [*reibō*] air-conditioning
バー [*bā*] bar
お風呂 [*ohuro*] bath
会計係 [*kaikei-gakari*] cashier
食堂 [*shokudō*] dining room
ダイニングルーム [*daining-g rūm*]
　dining room
飲み水 [*nomi-mizu*] drinking water
飲料水 [*inryō-sui*] drinking water
クリーニング [*kurīning-g*]
　dry cleaning
非常口 [*hijō-guchi*] emergency exit
消火器 [*shōka-ki*] fire extinguisher
二階 [*ni-kai*] (UK) first floor,
　(USA) second floor
一階 [*ik-kai*] (UK) ground floor,
　(USA) first floor
暖房 [*dambō*] heating
温泉 [*onsen*] hot spring

ホテル [*hoteru*] hotel
旅館 [*ryokan*] Japanese-style inn
和室 [*washits*] Japanese-style room
日本交通公社 [*Nihon kōtsū kōsha*]
    Japan Travel Bureau
エレベーター [*erebētā*] lift, elevator
ロビー [*robī*] lobby
ラウンジ [*raunji*] lounge
男 [*otoko*] men
立入禁止 [*tachi-iri-kinshi*] no entry
民宿 [*minshku*] people's inn
引く [*hik*] pull
押す [*oss*] push
受付 [*uketske*] reception
フロント [*huronto*] reception
レストラン [*restoran*] restaurant
室 [*heya*] room
ルームサービス [*rūm sābiss*]
    room service
電話室 [*denwa-shits*]
    telephone booth
お手洗い [*otearai*] toilet, rest room
自動販売器 [*jidō-hambai-ki*]
    vending machine
洋室 [*yōshits*] Western-style room
女 [*on-na*] women

LIFTS/ELEVATORS

二階 [*ni-kai*] (UK) first floor,
    (USA) second floor
階 [*-kai*] floor, stor(e)y
一階 [*ik-kai*] (UK) ground floor,
    (USA) first floor
地階 [*chi-kai*] basement
定員 [*tei-in*] capacity
閉 [*hei*] close
下 [*shta*] down
非常停止 [*hijō-teishi*] emergency
    stop
非常電話 [*hijō-denwa*]
    emergency telephone
満員 [*man'in*] full
エレベーター [*erebētā*] lift, elevator

開 [*kai*] open
故障 [*koshō*] out of order
上 [*ue*] up

MEDICAL

救急車 [*kyūkyūsha*] ambulance
血液 [*ketsu-eki*] blood
献血 [*kenkets*] blood donation
診療所 [*shinryo-jo*] clinic
診療 [*shinryō*] consultation
診療時間 [*shinryō-jikan*]
    consultation hours
歯医者 [*haisha*] dentist
歯科 [*shka*] dentistry
…科 [*... ka*] ... department
医者 [*isha*] doctor
耳鼻咽喉科 [*jibiinkōka*]
    ear, nose and throat department
眼科 [*ganka*] eye department
病院 [*byōin*] hospital
産婦人科 [*sanhujinka*]
    obstetrics and gyn(a)ecology
小児科 [*shōnika*] p(a)ediatrics
赤十字 [*sekijūji*] Red Cross
医院 [*īn*] (small) hospital
外科 [*geka*] surgery (*operations*)

MEDICINE LABELS

食後 [*shokugo*] after meals
就寝前 [*shūshin-zen*]
    before going to bed
食前 [*shokuzen*] before meals
食間 [*shok-kan*] between meals
服用方法 [*hukuyō-hōhō*]
    directions for oral use
匙 [*saji*] spoonfuls
錠剤 [*jōzai*] tablets
一日…錠 [*ichinichi ... jō*]
    ... tablets a day
一日…回 [*ichinichi ... kai*]
    ... times a day

MONTHS

一月 [*ichi-gats*] January
二月 [*ni-gats*] February
三月 [*san-gats*] March
四月 [*shi-gats*] April
五月 [*go-gats*] May
六月 [*roku-gats*] June
七月 [*shchi-gats*] July
八月 [*hachi-gats*] August
九月 [*ku-gats*] September
十月 [*jū-gats*] October
十一月 [*jū-ichi-gats*] November
十二月 [*jū-ni-gats*] December
一ヶ月 [*ik-ka-gets*] one month

MOVIE THEATERS *see* CINEMAS

NIGHT LIFE

ディスコ [*disko*] disco
ホステスバー [*hostess-bā*] hostess bar
ナイトクラブ [*naitokurab*] nightclub
トルコ風呂 [*toruko-buro*]
   Turkish bath
ソープランド [*sōpurando*]
   Turkish bath

NOTICES AND SIGNS IN SHOPS

バーゲン [*bāgen*] bargain(s)
レジ [*reji*] cash point
御会計 [*okaikei*] cashier
休日 [*kyūjits*] closed
非常口 [*hijō-guchi*] emergency exit
御歳暮 [*oseibo*] end-of-year presents
エスカレーター [*eskarētā*] escalator
…階 [*... -kai*] floor
大売出し [*ōuridashi*] grand sale
案内 [*an-nai*] information
エレベーター [*erebētā*] lift, elevator
御中元 [*ochūgen*]
   mid-summer presents
営業中 [*eigyō-chū*] open for business

お手をふれないでください
   [*ote o hurenaide kudasai*]
   please do not touch
セール [*sēru*] sale
特別価格 [*tokubets kakak*]
   special price
お手洗い [*otearai*] toilet, rest room

NOTICES AND SIGNS ON DOORS

自動ドア [*jidō-doa*] automatic door
カード可 [*kādo ka*] cards accepted
月曜定休日 [*getsyō teikyū bi*]
   closed on Mondays
日・祭日休み [*nichi saijits yasumi*]
   closed on Sundays and National
   Holidays
本日休業 [*honjits kyūgyō*]
   closed today
非常出口 [*hijō-deguchi*]
   emergency exit
入口 [*iriguchi*] entrance
出口 [*deguchi*] exit
定休日 [*teikyūbi*] holidays
開放厳禁 [*kaihō-genkin*] keep closed
カード不可 [*kādo huka*]
   no cards accepted
立入禁止 [*tachi-iri-kinshi*] no entry
関係者以外立入禁止
   [*kankeisha-igai-tachi-iri-kinshi*]
   no entry except for authorized
   personnel
開く [*hirak*] open
営業中 [*eigyō-chū*] open
年中無休 [*nenjū mukyū*]
   open all year round
引く [*hik*] pull
押す [*oss*] push
セール実施中 [*sēru jissh-shi-chū*]
   sale now on
閉じる [*tojiru*] shut

PLACE NAMES

箱根 [*Hakone*] Hakone
広島 [*Hiroshima*] Hiroshima
北海道 [*Hok-kaidō*] Hokkaido
本州 [*Honshū*] Honshu
伊勢 [*Ise*] Ise
鎌倉 [*Kamakura*] Kamakura
関西 [*Kansai*]
  Kansai Region (Osaka etc)
関東 [*Kantō*]
  Kantō Region (Tokyo etc)
神戸 [*Kōbe*] Kobe
京都 [*Kyōto*] Kyoto
九州 [*Kyūshū*] Kyushu
長崎 [*Nagasaki*] Nagasaki
名古屋 [*Nagoya*] Nagoya
奈良 [*Nara*] Nara
日光 [*Nik-kō*] Nikko
大阪 [*Ōsaka*] Osaka
四国 [*Shkok*] Shikoku
東京 [*Tōkyō*] Tokyo
横浜 [*Yokohama*] Yokohama

POST OFFICES

住所 [*jūsho*] address
あて名 [*atena*] addressee
航空書簡 [*kōkū shokan*]
  aerogram(me)s
航空便 [*kōkūbin*] airmail
電信 [*denshin*] cables
記念切手 [*kinen kit-te*]
  commemorative stamps
窓口 [*madoguchi*] counter
税関申告用紙 [*zeikan-shinkok-yōshi*]
  customs declaration form
税関告知書 [*zeikan kok-chi sho*]
  customs declaration form
速達 [*soktats*] express mail
外国人登録証明書
  [*gaikoku-jin tōrok shōmei-sho*]
  foreign residents' ID cards
用紙 [*yōshi*] form

身分証明書 [*mibun shōmei-sho*]
  ID cards
手紙 [*tegami*] letters
為替 [*kawase*] money orders
地方 [*chihō*] out of town
外国向け [*gaikoku-muke*]
  overseas mail
小包 [*kozutsumi*] parcels, packages
郵便局 [*yūbin-kyok*] post office
郵便貯金 [*yūbin chokin*]
  post office savings
〒 [*yūbin-kyok no māk*]
  'post office symbol'
  (*not a Japanese character*)
留置 [*tome-oki*]
  poste restante, general delivery
印刷物 [*insats-buts*] printed matter
現金書留封筒 [*genkin kakitome hūtō*]
  registered cash envelopes
書留 [*kakitome*] registered mail
往復はがき [*ōhuku-hagaki*]
  return-paid postcards
船便 [*hunabin*] sea mail
切手 [*kit-te*] stamps
普通便 [*hutsū-bin*] surface mail
電報 [*dempō*] telegrams
アメリカ向け [*Amerika-muke*]
  to America
イギリス向け [*Igiriss-muke*]
  to Britain
都区内 [*toku nai*]
  to other parts of Tokyo
他府県 [*ta-hu ken*]
  to other prefectures
円 [*en*] yen

PUBLIC BUILDINGS

美術館 [*bijuts-kan*] art gallery
領事館 [*ryōji-kan*] consulate
大使館 [*taishkan*] embassy
体育館 [*tai-iku-kan*] gymnasium
病院 [*byōin*] hospital
中学校 [*chū-gak-kō*] junior

high school
裁判所 [saiban-sho] law court
図書館 [tosho-kan] library
市役所 [shiyak-sho]
    local government offices, city hall
県/都/府庁 [ken-/to-/hu-chō]
    local government offices
    (for districts)
博物館 [haku-buts-kan] museum
郵便局 [yūbin-kyok] post office
小学校 [shō-gak-kō] primary school
保健所 [hoken-sho]
    public health centre/center
高等学校 [kōtō-gak-kō]
    senior high school
大学 [daigak] university

RENTALS

レンタカー [rentakā] car rental
貸自動車 [kashi jidōsha] car rental
時間貸し [jikan-gashi] hourly rental
距離払い [kyori-barai]
    payment by distance
時間払い [jikam-barai]
    payment by the hour
レンタルサービス [rentaru sābiss]
    rental service

REPLIES, THINGS YOU'LL HEAR

arigatō thank you
arigatō gozai-mass
    thank you very much
daijōbu dess
    I'm all right, that's all right
daijōbu dess ka? are you all right?,
    is it all right?
dame (dess)! don't!
dō-itashi-mashte
    you're welcome, not at all
dōmo thanks
dōmo arigatō thank you very much
dōzo (osaki ni) go ahead

gomen nasai I'm sorry
ī dess ka? is that all right?, may I?
ī dess yo
    that's all right/yes, you may
kek-kō dess arigatō
    that's fine thank you/
    no thank you
nan dess ka? what is it?
ōkini thank you (*Kansai dialect*)
onegai shi-mass (would you) please
shimpai shinaide don't worry
sumi-masen I'm sorry, excuse me
wakari-masen I don't understand
yoroshī dess yo
    that's all right/yes, you may

REST ROOMS *see* TOILETS

ROAD SIGNS

この先100メートル [kono saki hyak
    mētoru] 100 metres/meters ahead
この先100米 [kono saki hyak mētoru]
    100 metres/meters ahead
事故 [jiko] accident
駐車場 [chūsha-jō]
    car park, parking lot
満車 [man-sha]
    car park/parking lot full
注意 [chūi] caution
危険 [kiken] danger
回り道 [mawari-michi]
    diversion, detour
非常駐車帯 [hijō chūsha-tai]
    emergency parking area
非常電話 [hijō-denwa]
    emergency telephone
入口 [iriguchi] entrance
出口 [deguchi] exit
料金 [ryōkin] fee
有料 [yūryō] fee charged
一旦停車 [it-tan tei-sha]
    give way, yield

一旦停止 [*it-tan teishi*]
  give way, yield
交差点 [*kōsaten*]
  junction, intersection
本線 [*honsen*]
  lane for through traffic
踏切 [*humi-kiri*]
  level crossing, railroad crossing
最高速度 [*saikō sokudo*]
  maximum speed
国道 [*kokudō*] national highway
無料 [*muryō*] no charge
左折禁止 [*sasets kinshi*] no left turn
駐車禁止 [*chūsha kinshi*] no parking
右折禁止 [*usets kinshi*] no right turn
停車禁止 [*teisha kinshi*] no stopping
通行止め [*tsūkō-dome*]
  no through traffic
通行禁止 [*tsūkō-kinshi*]
  no through traffic
警察 [*keisats*] police
スピードを落せ [*spīdo o otose*]
  reduce speed
道路工事 [*dōro-kōji*]
  road under construction
工事中 [*kōji-chū*] road work(s)
急カーブ [*kyū-kāb*] sharp bend
一時預り [*ichiji azukari*]
  short-term parking
徐行 [*jokō*] slow
止まれ [*tomare*] stop
高速道路 [*kōsok dōro*] toll motorway/
  expressway
有料道路 [*yūryō dōro*] toll road
SCHEDULES *see* **TIMETABLES**

SHOP NAMES

屋 [*-ya*] ... shop/store
店 [*-ten*] ... shop/store
骨董店 [*kot-tō-ten*]
  antique/curiosity shop/store
パン屋 [*pan'ya*] baker

本屋 [*hon'ya*] bookshop, bookstore
喫茶店 [*kis-saten*] coffee shop
お菓子屋 [*okashi-ya*]
  confectioner's, candy store
デパート [*depāto*] department store
クリーニング店 [*kurīning-g-ten*]
  dry cleaner
電気店 [*denki-ya*]
  electrical goods shop/store
魚屋 [*sakana-ya*] fishmonger
花屋 [*hana-ya*] florist
果物屋 [*kudamono-ya*]
  fruit shop/store
八百屋 [*yao-ya*] greengrocer
食料品店 [*shokuryō-hin-ten*] grocer
金物屋 [*kanamono-ya*]
  ironmonger's, hardware store
売店 [*baiten*] kiosk
コインランドリー [*koin-randorī*]
  launderette, laundromat
市場 [*ichiba*] market
楽器店 [*gak-ki-ten*]
  musical instrument shop/store
酒屋 [*saka-ya*]
  off-licence, liquor store
めがね屋 [*megane-ya*] optician
質屋 [*shchi-ya*] pawnbroker
薬屋 [*ksuri-ya*] pharmacy
薬局 [*yak-kyok*] pharmacy
写真屋 [*shashin'ya*]
  photography shop/store
レコード店 [*rekōdo-ten*]
  record shop/store
古本屋 [*huru-hon'ya*]
  second-hand bookshop/bookstore
くつ屋/靴屋 [*kutsu-ya*]
  shoe shop/store
みやげ店 [*miyage-ten*]
  souvenir shop/store
スポーツ用品店 [*spōts-yōhin-ten*]
  sports shop/store
文房具屋 [*bumbōgu-ya*]
  stationery shop/store

スーパー [*sūpā*] supermarket
おもちゃ屋 [*omocha-ya*] toy shop
旅行会社 [*ryokō-gaisha*]
　travel agency
旅行代理店 [*ryokō-dairiten*]
　travel agency

SUBWAY *see* **UNDERGROUND**

SWEARWORDS

bakame! bloody fool!
bakayarō! damn fool!
chikshō! hell!
kisama! bastard!
konoyarō! damn fool!
kso! shit!

TAXIS

自動ドア [*jidō-doa*] automatic door
料金メーター [*ryōkin-mētā*]
　fare meter
空車 [*kūsha*] for hire, free
夜間割増料金 [*yakan warimashi ryōkin*]
　late night fare
回送 [*kaisō*] out of service
個人 [*kojin*] private owner
タクシー [*takshī*] taxi
タクシー乗り場 [*takshī-noriba*]
　taxi rank/stand

TELEPHONES

電電会社 [*Denden Kaisha*]
　abbreviation of Japan Telegraph
　and Telephone Co. Ltd.
電信 [*denshin*] cables
電話料金 [*denwa ryōkin*] call charge
電話代 [*denwa-dai*] call charge
大代表 [*dai-daihyō*]
　central switchboard
電話帳 [*denwa-chō*] directory
非常電話 [*hijō-denwa*]
　emergency telephone
内線 [*naisen*] extension

国際電話 [*koksai denwa*]
　international call
日本電信電話会社 [*Nihon Denshin
　Denwa Kaisha*] Japan Telegraph
　and Telephone Co. Ltd.
市内電話 [*shinai denwa*] local call
長距離電話 [*chōkyori denwa*]
　long-distance call
交換手 [*kōkan-shu*] operator
市外電話 [*shigai denwa*]
　out-of-town call
K.D.D. [*koksai-denshin-denwa*]
　Overseas Telecommunication
　Service
公衆電話 [*kōshū denwa*]
　public telephone
電報 [*dempō*] telegrams
電話 [*denwa*] telephone
電話室 [*denwa-shits*] telephone booth
電話番号 [*denwa ban-gō*]
　telephone number

THEATRES/THEATERS

切符売り場 [*kip-pu uriba*] box office
非常口 [*hijō-guchi*] emergency exit
帝国劇場 [*Teikok Gekijō*]
　Imperial Theatre/Theater
歌舞伎 [*kabuki*] kabuki,
　plays about Samurai period
歌舞伎座 [*kabuki-za*]
　Kabuki-za Theatre/Theater
国立劇場 [*Kokurits Gekijō*]
　National Theatre/Theater
狂言 [*kyōgen*] Noh comedy
能 [*nō*] Noh play
禁煙 [*kin'en*] no smoking
劇 [*geki*] play, drama
文楽 [*bunrak*]
　puppet theatre/theater
指定席 [*shtei-seki*] reserved seat
指定券 [*shtei-ken*]
　reserved seat ticket
席 [*seki*] seat

座席 [*zaseki*] seat
座席番号 [*zaseki ban-gō*] seat number
劇場 [*gekijō*] theatre/theater
お手洗い [*otearai*] toilets, rest rooms

TIMETABLES/SCHEDULES

到着 [*tōchak*] arrival(s)
出発 [*shup-pats*] departure(s)
発車 [*hash-sha*] departure(s)
時刻表 [*jikok-hyō*]
  timetable, schedule
経由 [*keiyu*] via

TOILETS/REST ROOMS

化粧室 [*keshō-shits*]
  ladies, ladies' room
男 [*otoko*] men, men's room
男子用 [*danshi-yō*] (for) men
使用中 [*shiyō-chū*] occupied
公衆便所 [*kōshu benjo*] public toilet
トイレ [*toire*] toilet, rest room
便所 [*benjo*] toilet, rest room
お手洗い [*otearai*] toilet, rest room
開 [*aki*] vacant, free
女 [*on-na*] women
女子用 [*joshi-yō*] (for) women

TOURISM

団体 [*dantai*] group
日本交通公社 [*Nihon kōtsū kōsha*]
  Japan Travel Bureau
予約 [*yoyak*] reservations
旅行会社 [*ryokō-gaisha*]
  travel agency
旅行代理店 [*ryokō-dairiten*]
  travel agency

TRAINS AND STATIONS

特急 [*tok-kyū*]
  abbreviation of limited express
大人 [*otona*] adult
前売券 [*mae-uri-ken*] advance

sale tickets
下車前途無効 [*gesha zento mukō*]
  after alighting, not valid for
  further travel
到着 [*tōchak*] arrival(s)
のりば [*noriba*]
  boarding platform/track
回数券 [*kaisū-ken*] book of tickets
…行き [*… yuki*] bound for …
新幹線 [*shinkan-sen*] bullet train
三号車 [*san-gō-sha*] car no. 3
小人 [*kodomo*] child
子供 [*kodomo*] child
コインロッカー [*koin rok-kā*]
  coin-operated locker
車掌 [*shashō*] conductor
出発 [*shup-pats*] departure(s)
発車 [*hash-sha*] departure(s)
行先 [*yuki-saki*] destination
食堂車 [*shokudō-sha*] dining car
方面 [*hōmen*] direction
東口 [*higashi guchi*] east exit
精算所 [*seisan-jo*] excess fare office
急行 [*kyūkō*] express
一等 [*it-tō*] first class
みどりの窓口 [*midori-no-madoguchi*]
  first-class ticket window
200円区間ゆき
  [*ni-hyaku-en kukan'yuki*]
  for destinations within the 200
  yen zone
グリーン車 [*gurīn-sha*] green car
  (first class)
団体 [*dantai*] group
左側通行 [*hidari-gawa tsūkō*]
  keep to the left
右側通行 [*migi-gawa tsūkō*]
  keep to the right
売店 [*baiten*] kiosk
一時預り所 [*ichiji-azukari-jo*]
  left luggage office, baggage
  checkroom
特別急行 [*tokubets-kyūkō*]

limited express

…線 [… sen] … line

お忘れもの承り所
[owasure-mono uketa-mawari-jo]
lost property office, lost and
found

遺失物取扱所 [ishits-buts tori-atskai-
jo] lost property office,
lost and found

お忘れもの [owasure-mono]
lost property, lost and found

荷物 [nimots] luggage, baggage

地図 [chizu] map

次 [tsugi] next

北口 [kita guchi] north exit

無効 [mukō] not valid

普通 [hutsū] ordinary

ホーム [hōm] platform, track

入場券 [nyū-jō-ken] platform ticket

私鉄 [shtets]
private railway/railroad

鉄道 [tetsdō] railway, railroad

予約 [yoyak] reservations

指定席（券） [shtei-seki (-ken)]
reserved seat (ticket)

定期券 [teiki-ken] season ticket

席 [seki] seat

座席 [zaseki] seat

二等 [ni-tō] second class

準急 [jun-kyū] semi-express

南口 [minami guchi] south exit

駅 [eki] station

駅長 [eki-chō] stationmaster

料金表 [ryōkin-hyō] table of charges

運賃表 [unchin-hyō] table of fares

乗換口 [nori-kae-guchi]
this way for changing trains

切符 [kip-p] ticket

切符売場 [kip-pu uriba] ticket office

…券 […-ken] … ticket

改札口 [kai-sats-guchi] ticket barrier

窓口 [madoguchi] ticket window

出札口 [shuss-sats-guchi]

ticket window

時刻表 [jikok-hyō]
timetable, schedule

二番線 [ni-ban-sen] track no. 2

電車 [densha] train

列車 [resh-sha] train

地下鉄 [chikatets]
underground, subway

自由席 [ji-yū-seki] unreserved seat

有効 [yūkō] valid

発売当日限り有効
[hatsubai tōjits kagiri yūkō]
valid only on day of purchase

経由 [keiyu] via

待合室 [machi-ai-shits] waiting room

西口 [nishi guchi] west exit

UNDERGROUND/SUBWAY *see also*
TRAINS AND STATION

地下鉄 [chikatets]
underground, subway

YOUTH HOSTELS *see also*
HOTELS

台所 [daidokoro] kitchen

キッチン [kit-chin] kitchen

コインランドリー [koin-randorī]
launderette, laundromat

売店 [baiten] shop

シャワー [shawā] shower

トイレ [toire] toilet, rest room

ユースホステル [yūss-hosteru]
youth hostel

Reference Grammar

The abbreviations used in this Reference Grammar are:

f	feminine
ind ob	indirect object
m	masculine
ob	object particle
pl	plural
qu	question word
sb	subject particle
sing	singular

NOUNS

Japanese nouns are very simple, having only one form. The addition or loss of a **-u** in the text is purely a matter of pronunciation and has nothing to do with grammar. There are no distinctions for number (singular/plural) or gender (masculine/feminine/neuter); nor are there any articles to bother about. Thus:

hon   a book, the book, books, the books etc
kuruma   a car, the car, cars, the cars etc
heya   a room, the room, rooms, the rooms etc

Do not worry about being misunderstood – what you mean will be clear from the context. Where necessary, you can be more specific by using numbers (see page 115).

As for a noun's grammatical function, whether a word is a subject or an object is not shown by the noun itself but by small grammatical words or 'particles' that come after the noun, for example:

the room   (*as subject*) heya wa
the room   (*as object*) heya o

See POSTPOSITIONAL PARTICLES (page 101).

PRONOUNS

PERSONAL PRONOUNS (I, YOU etc)
Japanese usually omits personal pronouns unless there is good reason to include them (for instance, to avoid misunderstanding). If you see someone getting ready to go out, you would ask:

where are you going?
[where to goes *qu*?]
doko e iki-mass ka?

since it is quite clear who you are talking about.

The general rule, then, is to omit pronouns where possible. If they do become necessary, use this list:

watashi wa*		I	**watashtachi wa**		we
anata	**wa**	you (*sing*)	**anatatachi**	**wa**	you (*pl*)
kare	**wa**	he	**karera**	**wa**	they (*m*)
kanojo	**wa**	she	**kanojotachi wa**		they (*f*)

*Or **ga**, see POSTPOSITIONAL PARTICLES (page 101).

Like nouns, pronouns do not vary according to their grammatical function – for direct objects, just change the **wa** to **o**, for example:

watashi o		me	**watashtachi o**		us
anata	**o**	you (*sing*)	**anatatachi**	**o**	you (*pl*)
kare	**o**	him	**karera**	**o**	them (*m*)
kanojo	**o**	her	**kanojotachi o**		them (*f*)

These lists of pronouns omit the word 'it'. This is because Japanese lacks an equivalent word. Consequently, you just leave it out, for example:

where is it?
[where is *qu?*]
doko dess ka?

here it is
[here is]
koko dess

it's me
[I is]
watashi dess

it's Tuesday
[Tuesday is]
kayōbi dess

it's raining
[rain *sb* falling is]
ame ga hut-te i-mass

If you really need to use something, you can use the word **sore**, but this is a demonstrative pronoun rather than a personal pronoun, and is nearer to the word 'that', as in 'what is that?'. 'It is expensive' is sometimes translated as 'sore wa takai dess' [that *sb* expensive is], but 'takai dess' [expensive is] would be just as good.

POSSESSIVE PRONOUNS (MINE, YOURS etc)
To form these, simply change the **wa** in the first personal pronoun list into **no**:

watashi no	mine
anata no	yours
kare no	his
etc	

For example:

it's mine	watashi no dess
is it yours?	anata no dess ka?
it's not his	kare no ja ari-masen

DEMONSTRATIVE PRONOUNS (THIS [ONE], THOSE [ONES] etc)
Do not confuse these with demonstrative adjectives (see ADJECTIVES). There are just three; like nouns, they are invariable in form:

kore	this (one)/these (ones)
sore	that (one)/those (ones) (*near person addressed*)
are	that (one)/those (ones) (*away from person addressed*)

this is mine/these are mine
[this/these *sb* I of is]
kore wa watashi no dess

I'll but that one/those ones (*near you, that you're holding*)
[that/those *ob* buy]
sore o kai-mass

that one (over there) is great/those ones (over there) are great
[that/those *sb* great is/are]
are wa sugoi dess

POSTPOSITIONAL PARTICLES

'Particles' are small words that always *follow* the word they relate to (hence 'postpositional'). They serve two principal functions:

1. To indicate whether a noun or pronoun is a subject or an object.
2. To act as equivalents of English grammatical elements like prepositions (to, from, with etc).

1. SUBJECT PARTICLES
To show that a word is the subject of a sentence, either of two particles, **wa** or **ga**, is used:

I'm an American
[I *sb* America-person am]
watashi wa Amerika-jin dess

the teacher went to England
[teacher *sb* England to went]
sensei ga Igiriss ni iki-mashta

The difference between these two is very subtle, but one way of looking at subject particles is to think of **ga** as emphasizing the subject of the sentence while **wa** de-emphasizes the subject in favour of what comes afterwards. Thus:

> ***this* one is mine** (*rather than that one*)
> [this *sb* I of is]
> kore ga watashi no dess

> **this one is *mine*** (*rather than his*)
> [this *sb* I of is]
> kore wa watashi no dess

> ***he* goes by train** (*not she*)
> [he *sb* train by goes]
> kare ga densha de iki-mass

> **he goes by *train*** (*not bus*)
> [he *sb* train by goes]
> kare wa densha de iki-mass

The **wa** often has the effect of setting part of the sentence aside, so to speak, allowing both **wa** and **ga** to be used in the same sentence:

> **it's raining today**
> [today as-for rain *sb* falling is]
> kyō wa ame ga hut-te i-mass

The following general guidelines will be of assistance in using **wa** and **ga**:

wa is very commonly used if the verb is **dess** or is a negative:

> **I am English**
> [I *sb* England-person am]
> watashi wa Igiriss-jin dess

> **that's expensive**
> [that *sb* expensive is]
> sore wa takai dess

> **there's no need**
> [that need *sb* there-is-not]
> sono hitsyō wa ari-masen

ga is very commonly used if the verb is **ari-mass** or **i-mass** (see ADJECTIVES), or if the subject is an interrogative:

> **there's a temple here**
> [here at temple *sb* there-is]
> koko ni otera ga ari-mass

> **which is the most interesting?**
> [which *sb* most interesting is *qu*?]
> dore ga ichi-ban omoshiroi dess ka?

> **who came?**
> [who *sb* came *qu*?]
> dare ga ki-mashta ka?

OBJECT PARTICLES
The object particle is simply **o**:

> **I (he etc) bought a car**
> [car *ob* bought]
> kuruma o kai-mashta

> **I saw a film**
> [film *ob* saw]
> eiga o mi-mashta

> **I drank sake**
> [sake *ob* drank]
> sake o nomi-mashta

INDIRECT OBJECT PARTICLES
To show that a word is an indirect object, use **ni**:

> **the teacher gave the student an exercise book**
> [teacher *sb* student *ind ob* exercise book *ob* gave]
> sensei wa gaksei ni nōto o watashi-mashta

2. The following illustrate some of the uses of the ten most useful remaining particles:

(i) **e**: motion towards

> **I'm going to Kyoto**
> [Kyoto to go]
> Kyōto e iki-mass

(ii) **made**: up to, until, as far as

> **until Wednesday**
> [Wednesday until]
> suiyōbi made

(iii) **kara**: from (either spatially or temporally)

> **from Osaka to Nagoya**
> [Osaka from Nagoya to]
> Ōsaka kara Nagoya made

> **since last Thursday**
> [last week's Thursday from]
> senshū no mokuyōbi kara

(iv) **ni**: used for time or location

> **on Tuesday**
> [Tuesday on]
> kayōbi ni

> **I live in Tokyo**
> [Tokyo in living am]
> Tōkyō ni sunde i-mass

(v)   **de**

   (a) by, with (in an instrumental sense)

> **I'll go by car**
> [car by go]
> kuruma de iki-mass

> **I'll order it by phone**
> [phone by order do]
> denwa de chūmon shi-mass

> **I can't eat with chopsticks**
> [chopsticks with eat-cannot]
> hashi de taberare-masen

   (b) a reason or cause

> **I can't because I'm ill**
> [illness with cannot]
> byōki de deki-masen

   (c) a place where some sort of activity occurs

> **I learned it at school**
> [school at learned]
> gak-kō de narai-mashta

(vi)   **to**

   (a) with (in the sense of accompanying)

> **I went with Mr. Tanaka**
> [Tanaka Mr. with went]
> Tanaka-san to iki-mashta

   (b) and (joining two nouns or pronouns, but *not* verbs or adjectives)

> **salt and pepper**
> shio to koshō

(vii)   **mo**
   (a) too, also

> **I want to go too**
> [I too wanting-to-go am]
> watashi mo ikitai dess

   (b) both ... and (with a positive verb), neither ... nor (with a negative verb)

> **I saw both the temple and the shrine**
> [temple and shrine and saw]
> otera mo jinja mo mi-mashta

> **I saw neither the temple nor the shrine**
> [temple nor shrine nor see-not did]
> otera mo jinja mo mi-masen deshta

(viii) **no**: this often corresponds to the English "s' or 'of'

> **Professor Okada's garden**
> [Okada Professor's garden]
> Okada-sensei no niwa

my book
[I of book]
watashi no hon

the car's steering wheel
[car's steering-wheel]
kuruma no handoru

This leads to its common use in prepositional phrases like 'in the room', 'on the table' etc:

in the room
[room's inside]
heya no naka

on the table
[table's top]
tēburu no ue

(ix)   **ka**: used to transform statements into questions

that's yours
[that *sb* you of is]
sore wa anata no dess

is that yours?
[that *sb* you of is *qu*?]
sore wa anata no dess ka?

(x)   **ne**: used as equivalent to English tags like 'isn't it?', 'haven't we?' etc:

it's yours, isn't it?
[you of is *tag*]
anata no dess ne

you bought it, didn't you?
[bought *tag*]
kai-mashta ne

VERBS

Verbs in Japanese remain the same regardless of number and person. So, for example:

iki-mass	means	I go
		you go
		he goes
		we go
		etc

There are only two basic tenses in Japanese:

PRESENT		PAST	
tabe-mass	I, you etc eat	**tabe-mashta**	I, you etc ate
yobi-mass	I, you etc call	**yobi-mashta**	I, you etc called

FUTURE
Because there is no real future tense, the present is used in its place:

> **I'll do it tomorrow**
> [tomorrow do]
> ashta shi-mass

The suffixes used above (**-mass** and **-mashta**) can be used for all verbs in normal, polite speech. (The only exception to this is the verb **dess** – see below).

A shorter, less polite form, the 'plain' form, is the form usually found in dictionaries (and is the form generally used in casual speech to friends and family members). The plain forms of the above verbs are **taberu** and **yobu**. These two represent the two basic verb-types of Japanese, each of which has, for our purposes, three patterns: Pattern A, Pattern B, Pattern C. All the verb forms you are most likely to need can be created from these patterns.

Most verbs ending in **-iru** and **-eru** are TYPE 1 verbs (e.g. **miru** and **taberu**). The seven exceptions to TYPE 1 verbs are **hairu** (enter), **hashiru** (run), **iru** (need), **kaeru** (return), **kagiru** (limit), **kiru** (cut) and **shiru** (know). These follow the TYPE 2 pattern.

All other verbs are TYPE 2 verbs. The nine possible endings for TYPE 2 verbs are shown in the following nine verbs: **yobu** (call), **yomu** (read), **shinu** (die), **oyogu** (swim), **uru** (sell), **warau** (laugh), **kak** (write), **hanass** (speak), **mats** (wait).

PATTERN A
This pattern gives us the basic stem, from which we make simple verbs and verbs of wanting and suggesting.

TYPE 1:   remove **-ru** (thus **mi-** and **tabe-**)

TYPE 2:   change **-u** to **-i** (**yobi-**, **yomi-**, **shini-** etc)
change **-k** to **-ki** (**kaki-**)
change **-ss** to **-shi*** (**hanasht-**)
change **-ts** to **-chi** (**machi-**)

* This final **-i** disappears before a **-t-**.

To these stems add the following suffixes:

	POSITIVE	NEGATIVE
simple present	**-mass**	**-masen**
simple past	**-mashta**	**-masen deshta**
wanting present	-tai dess	-taku* nai dess
wanting past	-takat-ta dess	-taku* nakat-ta dess
suggesting	**-mashō**	--

* This final **-u** disappears in spoken Japanese.

For example:

mi-mass	I see it
tabe-masen deshta	I didn't eat
kaki-tai dess	I want to write, I'd like to write
hanash-tak nakat-ta dess	I didn't want to speak
machi-mashō	let's wait

PATTERN B
This pattern gives the so-called 'participle', and is used in forming progressive tenses ('is going' etc), polite commands ('do it please' etc) and requests of various kinds ('could you do it please?', 'may I do it?' etc):

TYPE 1:   add **-te** to the Pattern A stem (**mite, tabete**)

TYPE 2:   change **-k** to **-ite*** (**kak** to **kaite**)
change **-gu** to **-ide** (**oyogu** to **oyoide**)
change **-bu, -mu, -nu** to **-nde** (**yobu** to **yonde** etc)
change **-ru, -ts,** (any vowel +) **-u** to **-t-te** (**uru** to **ut-te, warau** to **warat-te** etc)
change **-ss** to **-shte** (**dass** to **dashte**)

* One exception: **-ik** becomes **-it-te**.

The participle can be used in combination with the following:

	POSITIVE	NEGATIVE
progressive present	**+ i-mass**	**+ i-masen**
progressive past	**+ i-mashta**	**+ i-masen deshta**
polite commands	**+ kudasai**	--
requests (of others)	**+ kure-masen ka?**	--
requests (of self)	**+ mo ī dess ka?**	--
must not	**+ wa ike-masen**	--

For example:

he is waiting for a taxi
takshī o mat-te i-mass

he wasn't swimming
oyoide i-masen deshta

write it please
kaite kudasai

would you open the window please?
mado o akete kure-masen ka?

can/may I open the window?
mado o akete mo ī dess ka?

you must not swim
oyoide wa ike-masen

To form a negative imperative (to say 'don't ...') the stem must end in **-a**, **-e**, or **-i**. The correct ending simply has to be learnt with each verb. This form is then used with the prefix **-naide**, for example:

please don't wait	mata-naide kudasai
please don't say anything	nani mo iwa-naide kudasai
please don't speak English	Eigo o hanasa-naide kudasai

Two exceptions are:

kuru	(to come)	**ko-naide**	don't come
suru	(to do)	**shi-naide**	don't do

PATTERN C
This pattern is very easily formed from Pattern B. Simply change final **-e** to **-a** (**kaite** to **kaita**, **oyoide** to **oyoida** etc). This new form (which is, in fact, a plain past form and cannot therefore be used as a main verb in polite language) may be used to express the perfect tense ('I have eaten' etc) by adding the phrase:

koto ga ari-mass (*positive*)
or **koto ga ari-masen** (*negative*)

For example:

I've seen the shrine
jinja o mita koto ga ari-mass

have you not met him?
kare ni at-ta koto ga ari-masen ka?

THE VERB 'TO BE'
There are two types of verb for 'to be':

(i) for expressing a permanent quality or the identity of something.

(ii) for expressing position or existence.

For (i) use the following:

	POSITIVE	NEGATIVE
present	**dess**	**ja ari-masen**
past	**deshta**	**ja ari-masen deshta**

For example:

I am English
Igiriss-jin dess

it wasn't a present
omiyage ja ari-masen deshta

Note: with these four forms no particles are used.

For (ii) use:

	INANIMATE SUBJECTS		ANIMATE SUBJECTS	
	positive	negative	positive	negative
present	**ari-mass**	**ari-masen**	**i-mass**	**i-masen**
past	**ari-mashta**	**ari-masen deshta**	**i-mashta**	**i-masen deshta**

For example:

there are no bananas
banana wa ari-masen

it was on the table
tēburu no ue ni ari-mashta

is Mr. Kimura in?
Kimura-san wa i-mass ka?

no, he isn't
i-masen

Note also that **ari-mass** and **ari-masen** may be used to translate 'have' in the sense of 'I have got':

have you got any money?
okane ga ari-mass ka?

no, I haven't
īe, ari-masen

IRREGULAR VERBS
Two of the commonest verbs in the language, **suru** (do) and **kuru** (come), are irregular in some of their forms:

	SURU	KURU
Pattern A	**shi-***	**ki-**
Pattern B	**shte**	**kite**
Pattern C	**shta**	**kita**

For example:

I'll do it	shi-mass
have you done it?	shta koto ga ari-mass ka?
please do it	shte kudasai
he came yesterday	kinō ki-mashta

* This **-i-** disappears before a **-t-**:

shtai dess   I want to do it

NEGATIVES

There is no simple negative word like 'not' in Japanese. Instead the **-mass** suffix changes to **-masen** and the **-tai** suffix to **-tak nai** (see page 107). (This is why all the verbs in the 3 patterns had to be given separate positive/negative listings.)

I'll buy it	kai-mass
I won't buy it	kai-masen
I want to eat sushi	sushi ga tabe-tai dess
I don't want to eat sushi	sushi wa tabe-tak nai dess

Similarly, there is no single Japanese word for negative ideas like 'nobody', 'no-one', 'never', 'none', 'neither', 'nor', all of which must be accompanied in Japanese by a negative verb and the change of subject particles **ga** or **wa** into **mo**.

nobody came	dare mo ki-masen deshta
none of them is expensive	dore mo takaku ari-masen
I want to buy neither	kore mo sore mo kaitak
this one nor that one	nai dess

The same type of negative construction is used for Japanese expressions involving 'hardly':

I hardly ever go	hotondo iki-masen

Some positive constructions become negative when translated into Japanese. For example:

he may be upstairs	ue ni iru kamo shire-masen
I may buy it	kau kamo shire-masen

ADJECTIVES

Japanese adjectives differ more from their English counterparts than any other part of grammar; many, indeed, are more like verbs since they have separate forms for present and past, positive and negative. There are two types of Japanese adjective:

TYPE 1

These end in **-ai**, **-ii**, **-oi** or **-ui**, for example:

akai	is red	**oishii**	is delicious
shiroi	is white	**samui**	is cold

To find the stem, simply remove the final **-i**; to find the right form, add the following suffixes:

PRESENT POSITIVE   PAST POSITIVE

aka-	**-i**	(is red)	**-kat-ta**	(was red)
oishi-*	**-i**	(is delicious)	**-kat-ta**	(was delicious)
shiro-	**-i**	(is white)	**-kat-ta**	(was white)
samu-	**-i**	(is cold)	**-kat-ta**	(was cold)

PRESENT NEGATIVE   PAST NEGATIVE

aka-	**-ku** nai	(is not red)	**-ku** nakat-ta	(was not red)
oishi-*	**-ku nai**	(is not delicious)	**-ku nakat-ta**	(was not delicious)
shiro-	**-ku nai**	(is not white)	**-ku nakat-ta**	(was not white)
samu-	**-ku nai**	(is not cold)	**-ku nakat-ta**	(was not cold)

*   This **-i** disappears before a **-k-**.
** This final **-u** may disappear in ordinary conversation.

These are all plain forms: to make them polite, add **dess**:

it is red
[is-red (polite)]
akai dess

I saw a red book
[is-red book *ob* saw]
akai hon' o mi-mashta

this rice is not very tasty
[this rice *sb* not-delicious (polite)]
kono gohan wa oishku nai dess

TYPE 2

These are more like English adjectives – they have no verb-like character and do not change form; they are marked in the text by **na**, for example:

kirei (na)

If this type of adjective appears before a noun, the **na** must be used:

a pretty woman   kirei na on-na

If it is used without a noun, the **na** is dropped and a verb put in its place:

she is pretty
[she *sb* pretty is]
kanojo wa kirei dess

Note that here, a sentence like **kanojo wa kirei** is not possible – a verb must be added:

POSITIVE		NEGATIVE	
PRESENT	PAST	PRESENT	PAST
dess	**deshta**	**ja ari-masen**	**ja ari-masen deshta**

For example:

she's not pretty
[pretty is-not]
kirei ja ari-masen

it wasn't strange
[strange is-not (past)]
hen ja ari-masen deshta

The particle **no** is also used to form Japanese equivalents of adjective constructions in English. When **no** is given in brackets in this book it follows the same rules as those for **na**. See also POSTPOSITIONAL PARTICLES (page 101).

COMPARATIVES AND SUPERLATIVES (BIGGER, BEST etc)
For the comparative use **mot-to** before the adjective:

it was more interesting
[more was-interesting (polite)]
mot-to omoshirokat-ta dess

For the superlative use **ichi-ban** before the adjective:

the most interesting film
[most is-interesting film]
ichi-ban' omoshiroi eiga

For '**more ... than ...**' use the following pattern:

A wa B yori ... dess
[A *sb* B than ... (polite)]
A is ... than B

tempura wa skiyaki yori yasui dess
tempura is cheaper than sukiyaki

For '**as ... as ...**' use the following pattern:

A wa B to onaji gurai ... dess
[A as-for B as same about ... (polite)]
A is as ... as B

shabu-shabu wa skiyaki to onaji gurai takai dess
shabu-shabu is as expensive as sukiyaki

For '**not as ... as ...**' use:

> **A wa B hodo ... nai dess**
> [A as-for B as ... not is]
> A is not as ... as B

> **meron wa kaki hodo yasuku nai dess**
> melon is not as cheap as persimmon

DEMONSTRATIVE ADJECTIVES (this book etc)

Do not confuse these with demonstrative pronouns (see PRONOUNS). There are three: **kono**, **sono** and **ano**. Like nouns they are invariable; they precede the noun to which they refer:

kono ryokō	this journey
sono mondai	that problem (*of yours, that you mentioned*)
ano densha	that train (*over there*)

The difference between **sono** and **ano** corresponds to the difference between **sore** and **are** (see PRONOUNS, page 101).

POSSESSIVE ADJECTIVES (my book etc)

These precede the noun and are identical to possessive pronouns (see PRONOUNS, page 101):

watashi no	my	**watashtachi no**	our	
anata no	your (*sing*)	**anatatachi no**	your (*pl*)	
kare no	his	**karera no**	their (*m*)	
kanojo no	her	**kanojotachi no**	their (*f*)	

For example:

my ticket	watashi no kip-p
your key	anata no kagi

ADVERBS

Adverbs are created from adjectives by changing the -**i** of Type 1 adjectives to -**ku***:

hayai	quick	**hayaku**	quickly
osoi	slow	**osoku**	slowly
karui	light	**karuku**	lightly
yasashii	easy	**yasashku****	easily

* Except before a word beginning with a vowel, this final -**u** often disappears in speech (**hayak**, **osok** etc).

** Since in spoken Japanese, the -**i**- between **sh**- and -**k** disappears, this -**u** will usually be lightly pronounced; the same happens with -**u** between **s**- and -**k**, **yasui** becoming **yasku** etc.

Type 2 adjectives become adverbs by changing **na** to **ni**:

kirei na on-na	**kirei ni utai-mass**
a beatiful woman	she sings beautifully
jōz na ekaki	**jōz ni kaki-mass**
a skilful artist	he paints skilfully

WORD ORDER

The basic word order in Japanese sentences is Subject – Object – Verb:

> **I am learning Japanese**
> [I *sb* Japanese *ob* learning am]
> watashi wa Nihon-go o narat-te i-mass

If more elements are included, then the order is:

Other material [if any] – Subject – Indirect Object – Direct Object – Verb:

> **I gave him that ticket this morning**
> [this-morning I *sb* him to that ticket *ob* gave]
> kesa watashi wa kare ni sono kip-pu o age-mashta

Remember that to make questions, you do not change the word order as happens in English; instead, simply add **ka**:

> **who gave him that ticket?**
> [who *sb* him to that ticket *ob* gave *qu*?]
> dare ga kare ni sono kip-pu o age-mashta ka?

Remember also that adjectives precede the noun they modify while particles and conjunctions follow the noun they refer to.

YES/NO

The basic words for 'yes' and 'no' are: **hai** (or sometimes **e**) and **īe** (or **ie**):

did you see it?	mi-mashta ka?
yes, I did	hai, mi-mashta
did he buy it?	kai-mashta ka?
no, he didn't	īe, kai-masen deshta

Many speakers, however, would answer simply by using the verb without **hai** or **īe**.

When the question is a negative one, however, **hai** and **īe** are used in a way quite contrary to English:

isn't it open?	aite i-masen ka?
no, it isn't	hai, aite i-masen
isn't it open?	aite i-masen ka?
yes, it is	īe, aite i-mass

NAMES AND TITLES

The Japanese have two names – a family name like Kimura, Suzuki or Okada, and a given name like Kentarō, Yoshio or Yōko (many girls' names end in **-ko**). The family name precedes the given name: Okada Yoshio.

The given name is rarely used except by family and close friends; whichever name is used, the suffix **-san** (Mr/Mrs/Miss/Ms) must be added (other suffixes do exist: **-sensei** for teachers and doctors, **-kun** for junior males, **-chan** for children). The polite **Okada-san** will be used even when directly addressing Mr (or Mrs) Okada:

> **aren't you going?**
> Okada-san wa iki-masen ka?

rather than: anata wa iki-masen ka?

COUNTING THINGS

Japanese has two sets of numbers from one to ten:

1	(A)	**ichi**	(B)	**hitots**
2		**ni**		**hutats**
3		**san**		**mit-ts**
4		**yon** (or **shi**)*		**yot-ts**
5		**go**		**itsuts**
6		**rok**		**mut-ts**
7		**nana** (or **shchi**)*		**nanats**
8		**hachi**		**yat-ts**
9		**kyū** (or **ku**)*		**kokonots**
10		**jū**		**tō**

Set A is used for measures of time and money, with the measure being suffixed to the numeral:

5 minutes	go-hun
3 years	san-nen
one o'clock	ichi-ji
ten yen	jū-en

* The choice is not always a free one:

April	shi-gats (not yon-gats)
9 o'clock	ku-ji (not kyūji)

Set B is used for counting objects; with this set, the number *follows* the object:

two pillows	makura hutats
seven apples	rin-go nanats

Above 10, there are no set B numbers – Set A is used.

The system as outlined so far will be universally understood. But there is another method of counting which the Japanese themselves tend to use. This involves a system of 'classifiers'. These classifiers are similar to the words 'sheets' or 'head' in the English 'two sheets of paper' or 'three head of cattle'. Some common classifiers are:

-dai	for machines, cars, bikes, stereos
-mai	for thin flat objects, papers, tickets
-hon	for cylindrical objects, pens, cigarettes
-sats	for books
-hai	for glassfuls or cupfuls
-tsū	for letters
-nin	for people

For example:

2 sheets of paper
[paper-sheets 2 classifier]
kami ni-mai

7 pencils
[pencils 7 classifier]
empits nana-hon

3 cars
[cars three classifier]
kuruma san-dai

A final note on numbers: whereas Western unit divisions (thousand, million etc) are made every three zeros, Japanese has a four-zero unit:

10,000
[one ten-thousand]
ichi-man

20,000
[two ten-thousands]
ni-man

33,000
[three-10,000 – 3-thousands]
sam-man-san-zen

1,000,000
100×10,000
hyaku-man

10,000,000
1000×10,000
is-sem-man

DATES

The Western system of counting years is common in Japan:

1987
[thousand-nine-hundreds-eight-tens-seven-year]
sen-kyū-hyak-hachi-jū-nana-nen

Equally common is the traditional system of counting from the start of the current emperor's reign. The Shōwa period (of Emperor Hirohito) began in 1926 or Shōwa gan-nen: 1st year of Shōwa. Other dates are for example:

1927 Shōwa ni-nen (2nd year)
1957 Shōwa san-jū-ni-nen (32nd year)
1988 Shōwa rok-jū-san-nen (63rd year)

The date is given in the order year-month-day:

15th November 1987
Sen-kyū-hyak-hachi-jū-nana-nen jū-ichi-gats jū-go-nichi
(or: Shōwa rok-jū-ni-nen jū-ichi-gats jū-go-nichi)

TELLING THE TIME

The hours are formed by using **-ji** after Pattern A numerals (see page 115):

ichi-ji	one o'clock
ni-ji	two o'clock

But note:

yo-ji	four o'clock
shchi-ji	seven o'clock
ku-ji	nine o'clock

A.M. and P.M. are expressed by placing **gozen** and **gogo** respectively before the number of the hour:

9 a.m.	gozen ku-ji
3 p.m.	gogo san-ji

Minutes are expressed by combining **-hun** with pattern A numerals (though again, there are sound changes):

one minute	ip-pun	**2 mins**	ni-hun
3 mins	sam-pun	**5 mins**	go-hun
10 mins	jup-pun etc		

Minutes *after* the hour are expressed by giving the hour followed simply by the minutes:

6.15	rok-ji jū-go-hun
5.25	go-ji ni-jū-go-hun

Minutes *before* the hour use the same pattern plus the word **mae**:

five to three san-ji go-hum-mae

For 'half past', just add **-han** to the hour:

half past nine ku-ji-han

There is no equivalent for 'quarter of an hour': just use **jū-go-hun** (15 minutes).

CONVERSION TABLES

1. LENGTH

centimetres, centimeters
1 cm = 0.39 inches

metres, meters
1 m = 100 cm = 1000 mm
1 m = 39.37 inches = 1.09 yards

kilometres, kilometers
1 km = 1000 m
1 km = 0.62 miles = 5/8 mile

km	1	2	3	4	5	10	20	30	40	50	100
miles	0.6	1.2	1.9	2.5	3.1	6.2	12.4	18.6	24.9	31.1	62.1

inches
1 inch = 2.54 cm

feet
1 foot = 30.48 cm

yards
1 yard = 0.91 m

miles
1 mile = 1.61 km = 8/5 km

miles	1	2	3	4	5	10	20	30	40	50	100
km	1.6	3.2	4.8	6.4	8.0	16.1	32.2	48.3	64.4	80.5	161

2. WEIGHT

gram(me)s
1 g = 0.035 oz

g	100	250	500
oz	3.5	8.75	17.5 = 1.1 lb

kilos
1 kg = 1000 g
1 kg = 2.20 lb = 11/5 lb

kg	0.5	1	1.5	2	3	4	5	6	7	8	9	10
lb	1.1	2.2	3.3	4.4	6.6	8.8	11.0	13.2	15.4	17.6	19.8	22

kg	20	30	40	50	60	70	80	90	100
lb	44	66	88	110	132	154	176	198	220

tons
1 UK ton = 1018 kg
1 US ton = 909 kg

tonnes
1 tonne = 1000 kg
1 tonne = 0.98 UK tons = 1.10 US tons

ounces
1 oz = 28.35 g

pounds
1 pound = 0.45 kg = 5/11 kg

lb	1	1.5	2	3	4	5	6	7	8	9	10	20
kg	0.5	0.7	0.9	1.4	1.8	2.3	2.7	3.2	3.6	4.1	4.5	9.1

stones
1 stone = 6.35 kg

stones	1	2	3	7	8	9	10	11	12	13	14	15
kg	6.3	12.7	19	44	51	57	63	70	76	83	89	95

hundredweights
1 UK hundredweight = 50.8 kg
1 US hundredweight = 45.36 kg

3. CAPACITY

litres, liters
1 l = 1.76 UK pints = 2.13 US pints
½ l = 500 cl
¼ l = 250 cl

pints
1 UK pint = 0.57 l
1 US pint = 0.47 l

quarts
1 UK quart = 1.14 l
1 US quart = 0.95 l

gallons
1 UK gallon = 4.55 l
1 US gallon = 3.79 l

4. TEMPERATURE

centigrade/Celsius
$C = (F - 32) \times 5/9$

C	−5	0	5	10	15	18	20	25	30	37	38
F	23	32	41	50	59	64	68	77	86	98.4	100.4

Fahrenheit
$F = (C \times 9/5) + 32$

F	23	32	40	50	60	65	70	80	85	98.4	101
C	−5	0	4	10	16	20	21	27	30	37	38.3

NUMBERS

○/零 [*zero, rei*] zero, 0
一 [*ichi*] 1
二 [*ni*] 2
三 [*san*] 3
四 [*yon*] 4
五 [*go*] 5
六 [*rok*] 6
七 [*nana*] 7
八 [*hachi*] 8
九 [*kyŭ*] 9
十 [*jŭ*] 10
十一 [*jŭ-ichi*] 11
十二 [*jŭ-ni*] 12
十三 [*jŭ-san*] 13
十四 [*jŭ-yon*] 14
十五 [*jŭ-go*] 15
十六 [*jŭ-rok*] 16
十七 [*jŭ-nana*] 17
十八 [*jŭ-hachi*] 18
十九 [*jŭ-kyŭ*] 19
二十 [*ni-jŭ*] 20
二十一 [*ni-jŭ-ichi*] 21
二十二 [*ni-jŭ-ni*] 22
二十三 [*ni-jŭ-san*] 23
三十 [*san-jŭ*] 30
四十 [*yon-jŭ*] 40
五十 [*go-jŭ*] 50
六十 [*roku-jŭ*] 60
七十 [*nana-jŭ*] 70
八十 [*hachi-jŭ*] 80
九十 [*kyŭ-jŭ*] 90
百 [*hyak*] 100

百一 [*hyaku-ichi*] 101
百二 [*hyaku-ni*] 102
二百 [*ni-hyak*] 200
三百 [*sam-byak*] 300
四百 [*yon-hyak*] 400
五百 [*go-hyak*] 500
六百 [*rop-pyak*] 600
七百 [*nana-hyak*] 700
八百 [*hap-pyak*] 800
九百 [*kyŭ-hyak*] 900
千 [*sen*] 1,000
二千 [*ni-sen*] 2,000
三千 [*san-zen*] 3,000
四千 [*yon-sen*] 4,000
五千 [*go-sen*] 5,000
六千 [*rok-sen*] 6,000
七千 [*nana-sen*] 7,000
八千 [*hass-sen*] 8,000
九千 [*kyŭ-sen*] 9,000
一万 [*ichi-man*] 10,000
二万 [*ni-man*] 20,000
十万 [*jŭ-man*] 100,000
二十万 [*ni-jŭ-man*] 200,000
百万 [*hyaku-man*] 1,000,000
二百万 [*ni-hyaku-man*] 2,000,000
千万 [*sem-man*] 10,000,000
二千万 [*ni-sem-man*] 20,000,000
一億 [*ichi-ok*] 100,000,000
二十四万三千五百九十六
  [*ni-jŭ-yon-man-san-zen-go-hyak-kyŭ-jŭ-rok*] 243,596